CAMBRIDGE LIBRARY COLLECTION

Books of enduring scholarly value

Music

The systematic academic study of music gave rise to works of description, analysis and criticism, by composers and performers, philosophers and anthropologists, historians and teachers, and by a new kind of scholar - the musicologist. This series makes available a range of significant works encompassing all aspects of the developing discipline.

Letters to Wesendonck *et al.*

William Ashton Ellis (1852–1919) abandoned his medical career in order to devote himself to his Wagner studies. Best known for his translations of Wagner's prose works, Ellis also translated Wagner's letters to family and friends. In this 1899 publication, most of the letters are those which Wagner wrote to the wealthy retired silk merchant Otto Wesendonck, who provided Wagner with generous financial support and whose wife, Mathilde, provided the words for the *Wesendonck Lieder*. Also included here are letters to the German writer Malwida von Meysenbug, who was also a friend of Nietzsche, and to the novelist Eliza Wille, at whose house in Zurich, a meeting place for the cognoscenti, Wagner was a regular guest. She later published her memories of the composer. Despite the stylistic idiosyncrasies of the translations, these letters remain of value because they capture something of the colour of Wagner's prose and personality.

Cambridge University Press has long been a pioneer in the reissuing of out-of-print titles from its own backlist, producing digital reprints of books that are still sought after by scholars and students but could not be reprinted economically using traditional technology. The Cambridge Library Collection extends this activity to a wider range of books which are still of importance to researchers and professionals, either for the source material they contain, or as landmarks in the history of their academic discipline.

Drawing from the world-renowned collections in the Cambridge University Library and other partner libraries, and guided by the advice of experts in each subject area, Cambridge University Press is using state-of-the-art scanning machines in its own Printing House to capture the content of each book selected for inclusion. The files are processed to give a consistently clear, crisp image, and the books finished to the high quality standard for which the Press is recognised around the world. The latest print-on-demand technology ensures that the books will remain available indefinitely, and that orders for single or multiple copies can quickly be supplied.

The Cambridge Library Collection brings back to life books of enduring scholarly value (including out-of-copyright works originally issued by other publishers) across a wide range of disciplines in the humanities and social sciences and in science and technology.

Letters to Wesendonck *et al.*

RICHARD WAGNER

EDITED AND TRANSLATED BY
WILLIAM ASHTON ELLIS

CAMBRIDGE
UNIVERSITY PRESS

CAMBRIDGE
UNIVERSITY PRESS

University Printing House, Cambridge, CB2 8BS, United Kingdom

Cambridge University Press is part of the University of Cambridge.

It furthers the University's mission by disseminating knowledge in the pursuit of
education, learning and research at the highest international levels of excellence.

www.cambridge.org
Information on this title: www.cambridge.org/9781108079525

© in this compilation Cambridge University Press 2015

This edition first published 1899
This digitally printed version 2015

ISBN 978-1-108-07952-5 Paperback

Wagner
Letters to Wesendonck

RICHARD WAGNER:
LETTERS TO WESEN-
DONCK ET AL. TRANS-
LATED AND INDEXED
BY WM. ASHTON ELLIS.

London: Grant Richards, 9
Henrietta St. Covent Garden,
London, W.C. 1899.

Translator's Preface

WHENEVER Richard Wagner wrote a string of letters to a friend, he unconsciously bequeathed to the world a twofold picture : one side of this picture, and naturally the more elaborate, presents us with a portrait of himself, a portrait taken from a slightly different point of view in every instance ; the other side, more sketchy in its outlines, gives us a silhouette of his correspondent, so characteristic that we can almost trace the individual likeness, though it is afforded merely by the line of topics chosen for discussion, and the master's special treatment of those topics. In the present collection, the sources whereof I will state in a moment, we have first the wealthy merchant and art-lover, with his refinement of taste and practical sympathy, ever ready to lend the artist a helping hand ; next the literary comrade, a lady of glowing ideals and wide political horizons, thrilled by the power that lay behind those earlier products of the master's genius, the Dresden set of operas and the Zurich prose ; lastly the kind mother of a family, accustomed to soothe the bursting heart of husband and sons, and playing the part of ministering angel to the artist in his direst straits, though a trifle ruffled when the path of genius took such unexpected turns.

To descend to particulars : the letters forming the first group in this little collection were addressed by Wagner to a friend whose acquaintance he had made at Zurich in 1852, and with whom and his wife he remained on terms of cordial friendship until his death, though we are not accorded any correspondence of a later date than 1870—a fact presumably to be accounted for on the ground that subsequently to that date the master's letters were necessarily of much shorter length, owing to the immense amount of penwork into which he was drawn by the increasing publicity of his movements and the ever-widening circle of his friends, while, on the other hand, Bayreuth itself soon formed a centre where word of mouth usurped the place of written line.—Had it not been for Herr Otto Wesendonck's assistance during a long crisis in Wagner's financial position, it is hard to conceive how the artist could have survived to compose his later works ; for Liszt was willing enough, indeed, but his income had been seriously diminished by his conflict with the Weimar theatre-management.   To Wesendonck, therefore, should be assigned a place no less important in Wagner's life, than to that miracle of a King, Ludwig II. of Bavaria, and that paragon of an artist, Franz Liszt ; though all three must rank below the daughter of the last-named.

The letters to Otto Wesendonck were originally published in the *Allgemeine Musik-Zeitung* (Berlin) for the year 1897, by permission of Frau Cosima Wagner and of Frau Mathilde Wesendonck, the widow of their recipient. Frau Wesendonck herself will be known to most readers as author of the words of those "Fünf Gedichte" which Wagner set to music in 1857 to 1858 by way of preliminary studies for *Tristan und Isolde*. One letter addressed to herself, and also published in the *Allg. M.-Ztg.*, I have included in this series ; of course there were more, but these she has not yet made public.—The letters to Herr Wesendonck have been reprinted, in the original German, as a little volume edited by Herr Albert Heintz and published by Otto Lessmann, Charlottenburg, at the end of 1898, for the benefit of the Bayreuth Stipendiary Fund.

The next group of Letters was published in *Cosmopolis* for August 1896, under the title "Genius and World," with explanatory matter by Fräulein Malwida von Meysenbug herself. This lady, now residing at Rome, is best known to the world by her "Memoiren einer Idealistin," an extract from which is given, with her permission, among the Paris letters. We shall renew her acquaintance in the "Letters of Richard Wagner to Emil Heckel" (to form a companion volume to the present one).

The third group made its first appearance in the *Deutsche Rundschau* for February and March 1887, together with some extremely interesting reminiscences by the receiver,—reminiscences whose only fault is, that they contain two or three inaccuracies in important dates ; otherwise they afford a very valuable picture of the master at two dissimilar epochs in his life. The house of Herr and Frau Wille at Mariafeld, near Zurich, was long a favourite meeting-place for men of light and leading.

Taking the present collection of letters as a whole, we may be prepared for a repetition of the time-dishonoured cry that Richard Wagner was "always wanting money." No doubt he was ; his works, like those of every other commanding genius, were far in advance of his generation, and therefore could never reap a reasonable profit until after his decease, whereas a regularly paid employment is scarcely conducive to creation on the grander scale, as Schopenhauer has remarked : " The highest efforts of the human mind do not comport with wage-earning : their noble character cannot amalgamate therewith " (*Parerga I.*), and again : " A man thus inwardly endowed asks nothing but permission to be entirely himself his whole life long, on every day, at every hour. When a man is predestined to, stamp the imprint of his spirit on the whole human race, for him there is but one happiness or misery, namely, to be able to develop his faculties to the full, and complete his works—or to be hindered from so doing. Accordingly we see the great minds of every age setting the highest of all values on free leisure " (*ibidem*). How does Wagner himself express this ? Turn to the letter of October 25, 1859, to Wesendonck : " Let me work myself completely out : Oh, had I nothing, nothing else to do upon this earth !

Rest! Rest! That the inner torch may burn soft and bright!... Let me but create the works I there was given, there in peaceful glorious Switzerland... they're wonder-works; let me finish them, but ask nothing else of me!"

And why had he left the peaceful refuge so recently conferred on him by his friend in Switzerland? These letters give answer more plainly and emphatically than might have been anticipated. The cause was —his first wife, Minna, née Wilhelmine Planer. This lady's groundless jealousy of Frau Wesendonck would seem to have been brewing for a couple of years, before it came to such a head that there was nothing for it but to quit the little home so newly entered by the Wagners. Writing to Herr Otto in July 1865, the master refers to "the disturbance which drove me from you six years back" (this should be "seven"), and says that that grief should have been spared him. With his customary chivalry, he makes but the slightest allusion to his domestic troubles (as in the letters of Sep. 10, and Nov. 30, 1856), but it is highly significant that after 1855 we have only *one* message sent by Minna to the Wesendonck household, namely, a joint inquiry after Frau Mathilde's health at the end of that letter of Nov. 30, 1856. Though Minna is often referred to in the Paris series of letters, not once does she send the Wesendoncks a greeting thence! There's a world of meaning in that silence.

Harsh as it may sound to say it, the merest justice to Richard Wagner's memory demands that it should be placed on record that during the latter half of their wedded life Minna hung like a thunder-cloud above her husband's head, continually discharging shocks that shattered his most cherished plans (half against her will), and filling him with dread of what might happen next. Even when finally separated, this luckless invalid's power for evil was undiminished ; and it is surely more than a coincidence, that the most peaceful years of Wagner's life commence precisely with the date of unhappy Minna's death. In fact, two of the recipients of this present collection of letters have given us an insight into the poor lady's character such as we men could not so easily have gained : Frl. v. Meysenbug in her " Memoirs of an Idealist " says that " from her total inability to understand the nature of genius, and its relations to the world, there resulted almost daily jars and torment in their intercourse, increased by the fact that the absence of children deprived them of the last means of reconciliation. Nevertheless Frau Wagner was a good woman, and in the eyes of the world the better half and principal sufferer. I judged otherwise, and felt the deepest pity with Wagner, for whom love should have built the bridge by which to reach to others, whereas it was only making his bitter cup of life still bitterer." Thus the spinster ; her judgment is fully endorsed by the matron. Frau Wille in her article in the *Rundschau* remarks : " In his earlier days Wagner assuredly loved this woman, though she was a thousand grades from being his equal. He now [1864] is thinking of her lonely life in Dresden."

So let poor Minna rest ! To be the wife of genius, how few can bear the brunt : in all the world but one was fit for Richard Wagner's helpmate, and at last he found her. That noble woman I now desire to thank for gracious permission to translate these letters of her husband's, while acknowledging my indebtedness to the editors of the three original groups for the bulk of the narrative portion of the text and footnotes.

WM. ASHTON ELLIS.

May 1899.

Contents

LETTERS OF RICHARD WAGNER
TO OTTO WESENDONCK

In the year 1852 Wagner and his first wife, Minna (*née* Planer) were still living in the Escherhäuser on the Zeltweg at Zurich. After four weeks of work at high-pressure the artist had completed the poem of " Die Walküre " on July 1, and on the 10th of that month set out for three weeks of recuperation in Southern Switzerland. From Pallanza he wrote to Herr Wesendonck the following letter on the 20th July :—

Most valued Herr Otto !—
        I really should be the most ungrateful man in the world, if I did not think of you to-day. Here I sit by the Lago Maggiore, smoking the first of your cigars of the gods upon my journey. It weighs on my heart that I was so rude as to leave Zurich without a farewell : God knows I could not manage it ! Tired out and in ill-humour, after I had turned my back on the Bâle drinkers' (I meant to say, singers') feast (to which I did not even go), I had nothing in mind but to get away—away—away ! I should only have plagued you with my temper. But now I have run through the Bernese Oberland, climbed Faulhorn and Sidelhorn, and at last trudged over the very dangerous Gries glacier

into the Formazza-thal, through which I came down
yesterday to Domodossola.   That last day's march
was decidedly the most glorious thing that ever
has happened to me !   From the regions of perpetual
ice, through a series of sloping valleys, gradually
to descend upon the most luxuriant Italian vegetation,
was something quite new to me !   I have laughed
like a child over the wonders so often described
and read, but never yet seen and tasted by me.
To-day I first find *rest:* hitherto I had always
been as though in chase : the most majestic world
of Alps to me seemed but the gate through which
I must pass, to taste delight at last.   With a true
sense of bliss I now look across the lake to the
plains !   Yes, there is the world that yet might yield
me sweet impressions.   The influence of the Italian
air on me is indescribable.   I pushed on yesterday
evening, and drove from Domodossola to Baveno on
the Lago Maggiore : how I felt with such an ever-
smiling sky !—I don't know whether I shall have
time to write to my wife to-day, but to-morrow I
must begin and fire at her to come and join me ; [1]
gladly would I have every one I'm fond of by my
side just now : would that you could come too !
To-day I go on to Locarno, and to-morrow to
Lugano.   However, I should like to return here
again with somebody.   I am very lonely : and it
begins to be a burden to me.

[1] On the 3rd August Wagner writes to Uhlig : "I sent for Minna to come
to Lugano : then with her once more to Lago Maggiore, over Domodossola,
Wallis, Martigny, to Chamounix, Mer de Glace, etc.—to Geneva, where I
found your last letter.   Now we are off home by Lausanne."

God of mercy, whatever am I stringing together ?
Don't take it badly ! Only one thing more : how
many people there are, of my acquaintance, whom I
heartily deplore for not enjoying their life more
finely than they do. Of course that doesn't apply to
you. But I wish I were a genius like Herr von
Flotow—writing operas like Martha, and doing—
just what I can not !

How goes it with Donna Mathilda's [O. W.'s
wife] studies in thorough-bass ? Let us hope she
will have finished her first fugue by the time I
return ; then I will teach her to write operas *à la*
Wagner, so that she may put her knowledge to some
use ! Afterwards you'll have to sing in them : we
can translate your part into English, by all means,
as you sing nothing but English !

See, this foolish stuff is the result of your cigars :
if I were to smoke another, I should go clean off
my head : how that would delight some people !—
God save your lordship ! Farewell, and if a cigar
should happen to make you feel lively, just write me
too (to Lugano—*poste restante*) ; only, mind you take
a better pen than I've got hold of !—Should you see
my wife to-day please give her my best love ; and
preserve a friendly recollection of

Your
Richard Wagner.

A letter of the master's of June 11, 1853, Zurich, contains the following reference to his approaching composition
of the tetralogy :—

— — Everything depends on my thoroughly re-freshing myself first, to gain the necessary youthful courage—after five years' pause in music-making—to set about my new gigantic task with zest and cheerfulness. I have to close a whole long chapter of my life, to begin a new, important one : for that I need fresh life-impressions! I want a certain saturation from without, that a goodly counter-pressure may make me turn my inside out with joy once more. So I must be quite unhindered, able to travel, enjoy Italy, perhaps even visit Paris again, and thereafter come to that agreeable rest which fails me at the present. The remainder will then arrive of itself. — —[1]

Soon afterwards Liszt came to Zurich on a visit, about which Wagner writes on July 13, 1853 :—

To-day I merely send you these few lines, dear friend, to thank you for your last letter and at like time give you a sign of life from myself.

A wild, exciting—but vastly beautiful week have I just passed through : Liszt left me only a few days back. A very storm of confidences raged between us : my joy at the unspeakably winning man was all the greater as I found him vigorous, a good stayer, and much better in health than I should have antici-pated. We had incredibly much to tell each other :

---

[1] The dots and double dashes correspond with similar indications in the German that certain passages have been omitted from the published copy.—W. A. E.

for it really was here that we first made one another's acquaintance, as I previously had spent no more than a few flying days in his company. So the eight days, that he was able to bestow upon me this time, were filled with so much matter that I now am almost stunned by it. Quite at the beginning I sacrificed my voice, so that Liszt had to do all the music thenceforth: he played incredibly! One splendid trip I took with him to the Lake of Lucerne, and finally he parted with the voluntary promise to return next year for at least four weeks. I hope you, too, will then be here! Now I can hold out no longer in Zurich: yet I still have a great festivity to surmount to-night. A monster torchlight procession, with music, singing and diploma of honour, looms before me. The reports about it have kept the town agog for the last eight days. To-morrow morning, however, I go away to St. Moritz: if the cure is got through satisfactorily, then on to Italy. Well-ruled paper for sketches is all in readiness, and before this year has run its course I fancy the composition of Rheingold will be completely drafted. To my most delightful surprise, Liszt thoroughly concurred in my own plan for the future performance of my Bühnenfestspiel: we have settled that it shall take place from the spring to the autumn of one year at Zurich; a provisional theatre shall be built for it, and what I want in the way of singers, etc., shall be expressly engaged. Liszt will collect donations for the undertaking from every quarter of the heavens, and is confident of being able to scrape the needful

money together. You see, we've settled no small
thing between us !

Now, I hope I soon shall have your news about
the Wiesbaden performance of " Lohengrin," which
seems to have passed off very well. Your message
about the " Tannhäuser" was very interesting to me,
and heartily I thank you for it. Yet it appears that
you were able to derive a good impression.

Next winter there probably will be much musicing of mine in Germany : inquiries increase to such
an extent, that I begin to believe in my growing
popularity. May Heaven, Dr. Rahn and St. Moritz,
only grant that I regain my health ; for the exertion
I see before me is great, and to feel my spirits equal
to it I must also recover full faith in myself. Much
—much do I expect from Italy !

Hearty greeting, best friend, to you and your
honoured family : rejoice me right soon with news
how you all are doing.

Your R. W.

Wagner went to Italy at the end of August, but fell ill
at Genoa and got no farther than La Spezzia, where, as he
tells us in his letter to Boïto (*Prose Works*, v. 287), there
came to him " the prompting" of his music for " Das
Rheingold" ; by the 12th of September we find him back at
Zurich, still unwell.

On the 21st October 1854 he sends Herr Wesendonck
the following whimsical message :

You see, honoured friend, we no longer need lack ;
what we long have striven for is now attained—we

are made an Honorary Member of the Netherlands Music-society.   Our first joint laurel-wreath I beg you to hang up in your counting-house : the sight of it will give you courage and endurance, as it already has much exalted me !

Your R. W.

THE Philharmonic Society's invitation to conduct the season's concerts in 1855 was accepted by Wagner chiefly on the assumption that he would thus be able to break a path for the later introduction of his operas, and particularly of "Lohengrin," into London "under the protection of the Court." How much his hopes were disappointed will be gathered from the ensuing letters. We then lost a splendid opportunity of distinguishing ourselves on the right side of the page, to say nothing of even founding a kind of "Bayreuth" in our midst; yet no one but a German could have cherished the idea of storming such a strongly-held citadel of prudery tempered by philistinism as the musical London of those days.

In March 1855 Wagner writes from 22 Portland Terrace, Regent's Park—

Dear Friend,

What I have to report to-day shall be addressed to yourself, to take this opportunity of telling you how thankful I am for your many friendly offices. Gladly would I write you in a better humour, as I know that news of my welfare could but rejoice your sympathetic heart : but even to reach that good end I'll make no use of lies, and therefore confess to you at once that, if you still nurse hopes of my earthly prospering, I can give those hopes but little nourishment. London is a very large and rich city, and the English are exceptionally shrewd, self-possessed and intelligent : but unhappy I have nothing to do with them ! Through their taking me for something quite other than I am, for a time, things will go on for a time without much friction ; and as I am by no means inclined to tear them suddenly from their illusion out of sheer vanity, I only hope that time may slip by rapidly. Once again : I have nothing to do here. If you ask, however, *where* I should have anything to do, I answer : There where I have to keep least company ! Here, on the contrary, I am advised to call on so-and-so, for instance Davison (*Times*), Chorley, etc.; I am told they are . . . indeed,[1] but have their influence, and that it would be a pity for me to let my abilities and talents run to waste here. I don't know what *you* think about it ; but *I* can't help thinking I have nothing at all to seek here, with all my talents, and for that I certainly don't need the introduction of those gentry.—If I were to wish to be installed here as conductor of the Philharmonic for a series of years, there's little doubt but that I could easily effect it, for the people see that I am a good conductor : but *that* would be all the delight I could

---

[1] Though the attacks of Davison *et al.* upon Wagner were savage enough, we must remember that the artist had at that time a certain London adviser whose tactics had been little calculated to prepare a pleasant reception for him, and whose opinion of contemporary English critics was, to say the least, somewhat melodramatic.

gain here ; beyond it there is nothing. Of any
particular interest in my operas and a good sound
German theatre, especially on the part of the Court,
there is not the remotest prospect, . . . and certainly
no one here arrives at any kind of interest in a thing
unwonted. This you may see by the people's very
nature. True art is something utterly strange to
them, and they assuredly are not to be caught by
anything but its incomings and outgoings. The
equanimity with which these persons listened to the
singing of a wearisome duet [by Marschner], for
instance, just thirty seconds after the close of the
"Eroica," was an altogether new experience to me :
all the world assured me that no one took the least
offence at it ; and exactly as the symphony, so was
the duet applauded. This by the way.—My only
source of satisfaction I had set in my intercourse
with the orchestra, which is highly attached to me,
and in the hope of fine performances themselves.
For one thing, I made much account of my having
been allowed *two* rehearsals for the next concert, because I hoped it would give me the opportunity of
taking the orchestra thoroughly in hand. But
yesterday's first rehearsal has dashed that hope as
well, since I have learnt to see that even *two* rehearsals
are too few for my object. After all, I had to pass
by many a weighty point, and recognise that I shall
never be able to retrieve it in one further chief
rehearsal—so that I shall have to content myself
with a very relatively good performance of the Ninth
Symphony. As regards my compositions from

"Lohengrin," this time I have felt to my great
distress what a mournful thing it is for me to have
to keep appearing before the public with such absolutely meagre extracts from this work : I seemed to
myself quite absurd, as I know how little the people
can learn of me and my work from these sample
snips with which I already am travelling just like a
commis voyageur. And to think that it is my best
years that I thus am spending on a wholly cramped
and shut-off sphere of artistic action! I would far
rather renounce all attempt at outward action, for *I
alone* can feel the torture of it! Under such circumstances the only satisfaction left me, would be to
have done something for my outward lot : it would
be a good thing for me if I could. But how, unless
by stealing? How fat my purse will grow on my
concert-honorarium, we shall see ; in spite of my
dear apartment, I have no absolute extravagance in
view, and consequently hope to save. But, for this
and every time, that's all! An Act of Parliament
was lately passed, according to which there is to be
no more copyright in works that have already
appeared abroad: only for such as, written in
England or for England, make their first appearance
here. So the first thing to greet me here was an
exquisite translation of the *Star of Eve* and
Lohengrin's Rebuke to Elsa, published by Ewer ;
and I am informed that a further complete selection
of my vocal pieces is contemplated in the immediate
future. Everyone seems to have the right to reprint
them as he pleases. Consequently I very much

regret the " carriage " I recently paid for getting these things sent to me in England.   Dearest friend, give up any idea of making me "independent"; all my life I shall remain a lump—that is to say, in the English meaning—and therefore can only wish that no one, in his turn, will depend on me; for whoever depends on me will not get along very easily. That's the long and the short of it! Perhaps, however, I soon shall give up art entirely; then all will be well.   'Tis it alone that still holds me fast to illusions at times, which can have none but bad results for me.   Periodically it makes me a little light-headed, and you know that light-headedness is good for nobody, least of all for him who gives way to it.   Assuredly—but a little more—and I once for all shall be in the position to radically plug that source of all the foolishness in my existence. Already I have cause enough; the griefs my art itself prepares me, by far outweigh the rare entrancements it affords me.   It needs but little, nay, one sole thing, and I give this game up too : there then will be a likelihood, tho' of another kind than some might think.

I called on Herr B. in the city; the day after to-morrow he will send his carriage to take me to his residence outside the town.   At any rate you had given me a good introduction.   To tell the truth, both he and his belong to the party of the *Times*, in musical things as well : his wife is a connection of Mendelssohn's, as whose adversary people insist on regarding me, notwithstanding that I have been assured that they had never heard his overture to the "Hebrides" so well as under my direction. The B.'s, for the rest, have the reputation here of a very rich art(?)-loving house; we shall see. In any case I thank you for your friendly intention.

Otherwise, and up to now, my dearest London acquaintance is the first violinist Sainton, a Toulousian, fiery, good-hearted and charming. He alone is the cause of my summons to London. He has lived here for years in the most intimate friendship with a German, Lüders; the latter had read my art-writings, and they prepossessed him so much in my favour that he communicated them to Sainton as well as possible, and both came to the conclusion that I *must* be an able man and no mistake; so when Sainton proposed me to the directors, and was asked how he knew me, he told a lie: that he had seen me conduct,—because, as he says, the true reason for his conviction about me would have been unintelligible to the gentlemen. After the first rehearsal, when Sainton embraced me in an ecstasy, I could not help calling him a *téméraire* who might think himself lucky he hadn't been found out this time. This man is most agreeable to me. After yesterday's rehearsal, noticing my great exhaustion and concern, he would hear of nothing but accompanying me home and waiting till I had changed my clothes, when he countermanded my solitary house-dinner and marched me off to his rooms, where I dined quite comfortably with him and Lüders *en garçon*, till I grew of somewhat better humour. Such a man

in London, among the English, is a perfect oasis in
the desert. Anything more objectionable than the
genuine English stamp, on the other hand, I cannot
conceive : they one and all have the type of the
sheep ; and just as certain as the instinct of the sheep
for finding out its fodder on the meadow, is the
Englishman's practical sense ; his fodder he finds, to
be sure, but the whole lovely field, with the blue
heavens above it, unfortunately, is non-extant for his
organ of perception. Amid them, then, how miserable must anyone feel who only sees the field and
sky, but, alas! is bad at spying out the clover.

I am also very pleased with a young musician,
Klindworth, introduced to me by Liszt : if the
fellow only had a tenor voice, I should ·carry him off
without conditions, for he otherwise has everything,
and especially the whole exterior, for Siegfried. For
the rest, I now have a splendid Erard grand in the
house ; I had to have a standing-desk, for writing at,
expressly made for me by a carpenter : nowhere was
such a thing to be got ready-made. So I am set up
for my work since a few days back, but I have only
been able to make a poor beginning as yet ; the
interruption was too great and violent : at the first
my composition [*Walküre*] had become a total
stranger to me. Let us hope I shall find myself
again—or am I to give it up entirely ?

My God, what a jumble I'm writing you ; see
what you can make of it.—Your cigar-case is
regularly filled for me now by Sainton with excellent
wares.

I am hoping much for fine spring weather; my chilled condition will certainly not yield before. I then should like to make a few excursions; yet I suppose I shall have to forego everything, not to derange my present system of the strictest economy by what at any rate would much increase my budget of expenses; for without a terrible amount of money one cannot get about at all here : that you don't seem quite to know.

Please give my best love to my wife, from whom I had a letter yesterday, and give her whatever of rational news you may find in this letter, to which I must refer her for to-day. She is to rest assured— please tell her this—that she is a thousand times better off at Zurich than I in London, and that I am simply looking forward to my return.

To aunt Wesendonck and cousin Myrrha[1] give my best regards : that everything goes well, splendidly and capitally—to be sure, that's what they ought to think. For the rest, you must greet your honourable Sunday guests, and tell the Baumgartners[2] that there is *gute Wy* in London too. A thousand thanks for your loyalty and hearty friendship; if you mean to give me up some day, let me know in good time; I then shall stay in London!— Farewell, and remain fond of

Your

R. WAGNER.

---

[1] Wesendonck's daughter, subsequently Frau von Bissing, who died in 1888.
[2] Wilhelm Baumgartner and his wife; a eulogy of Baumgartner's songs will be found in Letter 54 to Uhlig. *Gute Wy* is Swiss for "good wine."

Wesendonck's reply was answered by Wagner on April 5, 1855 :

Dear Uncle,

If you go on at this rate, you will soon advance to the rank of my *father !* I was on the point of writing you about everything, from the Creation of the World to the evolution of English Music, when your last letter arrived, compelling me to begin a little more promptly and precisely. So : What may be the meaning of *Punch's* witticism, I know not ;[1] but I can assure you that I have accepted no money on bills of exchange. On the contrary, after the second concert Mr. Anderson called on Sainton with the question whether he knew how they were to proceed about my honorarium, whereon S. answered him : "How should I know? *Faîtes ce que vous voulez !*" Thereupon Mr. Anderson sent me a cheque for £50 as fee for the first two concerts, which I cashed at once, and expect to manage with for a long while yet. Consequently what *Punch* may mean need as little disquiet you as it concerns myself : neither has anybody said a word to me about it, nor had I myself yet read it. Perhaps I shall find out the meaning, and then will tell you.

Well, let us get on from English business to English music ; by which—as you will have gathered from Punch—one has likewise to understand nothing

---

[1] On March 31, 1855, *Punch* gave birth to the following :—"A Wag on Wagner.—We do not know what Herr Wagner's new musical theory may consist of, but we should say that 'the Music of the Future' must be composed principally of 'Promissory Notes,' made payable at two, three, or six months after date." A poor thing, but apparently *Punch's* own.

but business. You, also, seem to cherish the silent hope that I shall make English music after all, *i.e.* good business here. My letter about the second concert seems to have put that in your head again. Now, however unpractical and un-man-of-the-worldly I may appear to you, this time at least I would recommend a little sobriety and moderation to my enthusiastic friends, and beg them to expect nothing from me in the way of English music. It may perhaps be true, that my music pleased the public the other night; in fact, I find that still substantiated. Very good! But there's the end of it. Precisely in the same way as my music does the most wearisome stuff please the public; and exactly as my performances are applauded, are executions of the vilest sort acclaimed next day. So that I might consider myself to have soared to the height of the wretchedest music-making here, to be standing on a level with the other local heroes : that would be something! But it then would be a question of exploiting this standpoint to do precisely what the others do, in order to profit by their recognition; nay, I should have to be able to do it better than they, if I meant to gain anything by it. But there, dear friend, we come to the point where I am good for nothing. Under powerful guidance, and inspiring instruction, I should have to end by becoming a scamp among scamps : oh, what does a man not learn when he has a goal, an object before his eyes, that he imperatively must attain! But the worst of it is, with the best of wills I can spy out no *object*

to attain thereby. My *objects*, dearest Uncle, lie
somewhere else, and far as heaven away from all that
one can here attain ! I imagined you knew that.—
Never mind ! I am here, and will hold out to the
eighth concert :—beyond that, you surely don't expect more of me ? ?

You wish for newspapers ? Yes, but what are
they to contain ? Something to enable you to strew
sand in people's eyes about my successes here ? For
that the " Illustrated News " and " Daily News " alone
would be of use : these are furnished by the paid
secretary of the Philharmonic with laudatory articles
on the society's concerts, and consequently on my
doings also. A few other reporters find the tone of
Messrs. D. and C. too impertinent, and for that
reason give temporising accounts, in which I am left
with this or that good trait, but per contra this or that
bad one is not gainsaid. The capability of judging
me, or even impartially hearing what I give them to
hear, I disallow to them all. But, for knowing what
they want, the two aforesaid bear the palm : they
are paid to keep me down, and thus they earn their
daily bread, which is not so cheap in London as some
Americans believe.[1] Of the good-for-nothingness,
shamelessness, corruption and vulgarity of the local
press, everyone who lives here is so firmly convinced,[2] that—candidly speaking—I do not even
care to soil my hands by touching such a paper.
Those who understand anything, and really possess

---

[1] An allusion to Herr Wesendonck's former residence in the United States.
[2] See footnote to page 9.

an independent opinion, never mingle with this gang.
Thus I have been assured that a certain clumsy
veering on the part of the reporter to the " Morning
Post," after the second concert, was to have been pre-
dicted, and just because the " Times," etc., had fallen
so remorselessly foul of me, which forced the man
to be more prudent, as no one likes to quarrel
outright with the other ; for the time always comes
when they need each other's services. To the
editoriate of the " Times " itself, however, D.'s invective
appears to have been too strong and coarse ; wherefore it did not adopt his report on the second
concert. It is just possible that this unexpected
occurrence may restore a little courage to the other
papers next time, and a movement in my favour may
again be observable : possibly in this way, and with a
continued friendliness of the public proper, everyone
at last may turn round in my favour, to which
some manœuvre or other of the Philharmonic itself
—which is fighting for its own existence — might
contribute much ; possibly, therefore, you yet may
gain the right of saying : " I told you so. That's
the way of the world, and thus you come at last
to recognition." Everything is possible.—But I ?
What object have I with it all ? To conduct symphonies, which—to be candid—I only made my
métier at Zurich by way of exception, and to please
yourselves— : and what besides ? The Tannhäuser-
march and an overture of mine ? And then ? ? O,
it's good.—
My temper — not exactly sweet, as you see — by

no means comes of *my* having expected anything here, and now being disappointed : but through
others persisting in expecting something from an
utterly fruitless conflict of my nature with a nature
wholly alien to me. For my own part, I have already found the needful calm to look at the thing with
indifference and irony, and wait till it all comes to
end.   The fine weather will arrive, I shall frequently
go and see the wild beasts [in the " Zoo"], and
march home at last with a few pence saved.   What
would one more ?—

Ah, the lovely music that is made here!   The
other evening I was at a concert of the New Philh.
Soc. ; there you had a whole string of overtures,
symphonies, concertos, choruses, arias, and so on—
a perfect joy : all conducted by Dr. W., click-clack
till the thing ran out, which was fairly late : audience
applauding, as ever.   And in all the next day's
papers this concert was the finest of the whole
season ; directly after the second concert conducted
by me, precisely the same praise was dealt to this
concert by my most favourable reporter, as to mine.
Don't you think I ought to send you these newspapers ?

The real delight of the English, however, is
Oratorio : there their music becomes the interpreter
of their religion—*passez moi le mot!*   Four hours
long do they sit in Exeter Hall, listening to one
fugue after another in perfect confidence that they
have discharged a good deed, in reward for which
they will get nothing whatever to hear in Heaven

but the loveliest Italian operatic arias. It was this deep fervour of the English public that Mendelssohn gauged so well when he composed and conducted oratorios ; for which reason he now has become the veritable Saviour of the English music-world. Mendelssohn is to the English completely what their Jehovah is to the Jews. And Jehovah's wrath now strikes the unbelieving me ; for you know that, among other great qualities, the dear God of the Jews is also credited with very much rancour. Davison is the high priest of this wrath-of-God. What would Aunt say to my writing an oratorio for Exeter Hall ?

But I really must tell you something about the family B. It will be no small job, as this family is very large, lives at Camberwell,[1] eight miles from my apartment, and regularly assembles every Saturday[2] in the strength of about a quarter of a hundred heads. *He* is quite a nice man, bourgeois from head to foot, well-meaning and musical ; *She* is a connection of Mendelssohn's — shrewd, distant and — not bad ; daughters, sons, brothers-in-law, sisters-in-law, nieces and cousins, all sit down to tea after dinner—quite differently from your house—and get two or three other relations to play and sing to them, —naturally nothing but Mendelssohn. I have survived this experience twice already : for next Sunday, alas ! I have an engagement. What the quarter-of-

---

[1] Wagner spells it *Campervall*, which really is rather an improvement.
[2] " Sonnabends," strictly " of a Saturday," but perhaps it here means " Sunday evening."

a-hundred wants with me, has probably not grown clear to it as yet; perhaps it will discover in lapse of time.   I fancy B.'s benevolence will also find expression in a snug manipulation of the Press; if a right substantial article should come to light in this way, I will forward it to you.   At present the only object of interest to send you would be the programme of the second concert with the translation for "Lohengrin" and the explanation of the IX. Symphony.   But in this country such a thing—if not a journal—is prohibited *sous bande*, and in a letter it might come a little dear to you just now, when you are beginning to build your new house.   You see, I am passionately bent on frugality.—

God, what else had I got to tell you?—Really I can think of no right thing more.—Your long letter I have accepted with great thanks as the outpouring of the heart of a friend, and have mastered everything contained therein, with exception of the consolation, for which I no longer have a working organ. If I am to have good courage to live cheerfully for my inner vocation as artist, assurances of friendship such as yours will contribute no little to its revival; of that rest assured!—

Please thank Aunt kindly also, and assure her that I shall hold out.   Only, it goes slowly with my work :[1] I have almost entirely forgotten my composition, and often had to cogitate for long how I once meant this or that in it : here I have completely lost the inner memory.   The day before

[1] Scoring *Die Walküre.*

yesterday I very laboriously got through with the
first act, and already am contenting myself with the
hope of finishing at least the second act as well here ;
the third, however, I must save for Seelisberg, where
I unfortunately shall not be able to begin "Young
Siegfried " ; I shall be happy if I rediscover my work
itself there, and regain the courage for Young
Siegfried.   Believe me—I ought not to have come to
London !   That's the result, *quand on n'a pas
l'esprit de son âge*[1]—as you have given me to
understand.   Tut ! it will all turn out well, and—
I shall bring 1000 frs. with me : so the whole affair
has its reward ; how many a poor wretch brings
himself to the scaffold for much less !

Best greetings to my old woman : to-day she has
heard how I am lodged here.   Greet Myrrha too,
and—remain good to me, even if I can't send beautiful
newspaper-articles so soon !   Would that I could
say : To our speedy reunion !—

Your R. W.

The last letter from London is dated the 22nd May 1855,
the master's birthday :

Dear Friend,

A thousand heartfelt thanks for your charming letter ; it has given me great and genuine joy,
and thoroughly done me good !—I write you these
lines immediately after receipt of your letter, lest

---

[1] Probably a reference to chapter vi. of the first volume of the *Parerga*,
which Schopenhauer prefaces with a saying of Voltaire's : " Qui n'a pas l'esprit
de son âge, de son âge a tout le malheur."

any London atmosphere should blow up between its effect on me and my reply to you.—Believe me, my longing for home is great : I have neither rest nor pleasure, and if you figure to yourself a caged tiger ever prowling to and fro with but one thought, how to make its way through the rails and out,— you will have the picture of my daily disquiet.   Yet be assured that I do not blame you for advising me to make the London expedition.   I can imagine nobody who would not have advised it.   Only *I* should have known myself better, and *I* alone committed an inconsequence, which it is only just that I should smart for.   Were I Musician alone, then everything were quite in order ; but, unfortunately, I am something besides, and that's the reason of my being so difficult to dispose of in this world that it is impossible to obviate a thousand errors.   People have a deal of trouble with me : but thus much is certain,—money-making is not my business in the world, but *creating* ; and to enable me to do *that* undisturbed, the world would really have to care : yet the world, you know, cannot be forced, but does exactly what it has a mind to,—very much as I also should like exclusively to do.   So then we two—the world and I—are two stubborn-heads against each other, and naturally the one with the thinner skull must be broken in, which is the probable reason of my frequent nervous headaches.—Now you, dearest friend, have placed yourself between us two with the most excellent intention, assuredly to dull the shock : take care you don't also feel a little of it !

For that matter, the ground of my present dejection lies more in myself than in any unexpectedness of my experiences here. These merely confirm what I long had known before, and just as I latterly have aimed more and more at having to do with none but a few choicer spirits, whilst making no further demands on the public proper than at most the respect due to the Higher, so I have been able to console myself here with having won the true esteem of many individuals. What really disgusts and deeply wounds me, is chiefly inherent in the character of my function itself, inasmuch as I am obliged to play a rôle as concert-conductor and accommodate myself to the most inartistic views and habits, without even the satisfaction of getting my objections understood.— Well, my folly has been incurred, and for my wife's sake, who would have been terribly upset by the opposite course, I have determined to hold out, however bitter it may be for me. But at anyrate this last experience will teach me to rush into no inner discord of the kind again, and to keep entirely outside this humdrum musicing, so as to preserve all my strength for my creation. The stay here has been most hostile to my work; it has thrown me quite a whole year back, for I now feel my mind so exhausted that I shall content myself for the rest of this year with bringing off the " Walküre," and must save " Young Siegfried " for the next : this resignation is the only thing to give me a little peace.

To my great inner satisfaction—especially after your kind letter of to-day—I have no need to go any further into my relations with this place. You understand everything, and feel with me. O believe that I count that a gain ! The edge of every sorrow is soon blunted, when we find fellow-feeling for it : ay, this is probably the only source of all sincerest and most prospering love.

So let us simply think about a cheerful meeting ! With heartfelt joy I perceive that your dear wife is feeling well again. Give her my kindest thanks for the bass theme ; am I not, perhaps, to make a fugue upon it ?—Another purse from your dear wife ! Heavens ! Anyone who knew of my stock of purses would really believe that I had become a speculator on the " Bourse " with reference to your dear wife. I really shall never manage to wear them out ; and for very good reasons. Yet there still may be an opportunity of stuffing them all to the bursting-point ; —for I have just received a tentative inquiry from New York whether I should be disposed to go there on the special invitation of several societies—perhaps in two months' time—and personally pursue the propaganda of my compositions which has already been commenced by others with great success. So you see, the second edition of London is being prepared. At anyrate I shouldn't require to unpack at all in Zurich, to be able to go on to America at once.—Or shall I wait till you are installed on your new domain ? I see that you call it—Hochwyl ; it makes no difference to me ; I call it " *Wesenheim*," and so shall call it always : we shall see who gets the better of it, with his name ! For to-day you still must greet the

Hotel Baur and all that is therein, not forgetting wife and children!

God bless you! To our next meeting! To-day 5 weeks I start for home: may I find rest and refreshment among you!—A thousand thanks for all your friendship!—

Your

RICHARD WAGNER.

On the 25th June 1855, Wagner conducted the eighth and last Philharmonic concert of the season, which ended with an unexpected ovation on the part of the audience and orchestra ; as may be seen in his Correspondence with Liszt, where a letter of the 5th July tells us of the enthusiasm of an overflowing hall.

WESENDONCK and his family passed the winter of 1855-56 in Paris, pending the completion of his new villa at Zurich. They were still in the French metropolis when Wagner wrote on the 29th July 1856 from Mornex, on the Lake of Geneva, whither he had gone for a cure of the facial erysipelas which had been such a constant scourge to him during the recent winter :

Best thanks, dearest Friend, for your letter, from which I gather with delight that you all are well.—The further information about my project,[1] for which you ask, I can give you at present only in so far as concerns my own intention, since Härtels have not yet sent a definite answer. However, I can assure you that all the chances feared by you have been well foreseen in my proposals. Naturally, nothing will be published before completion of the whole ; only in case of my death ere such completion, or of my abandoning it, and consequently not observing

[1] See the letter to Liszt of 20th July 1856, which gives fuller particulars of Wagner's scheme to buy a little plot of ground to build himself " a small house with a garden, both removed from all noise " ; to procure the necessary funds, he was negotiating with Breitkopf und Härtel for the sale of the *Nibelungen* scores.

the specified (and fairly distant) term, would such a thing be allowed, to recoup the publishers for payment of the honorarium. The stage-rights would of course be reserved to myself.—Did you really think I was such a bad man of business, as to make no provisos about these points? Look! it annoys you to be always addressed as a business man, and you do me an injustice if you deny me any business-sense at all. Believe me, I too can count : unfortunately however, I always have such horrid things to discount, that it must not be accounted ill of me if for once in a way I miscount. Only give me such pleasant facts to recount, as must have happened now and again to yourself, and you'll be astonished at my accuracy.—My cure goes steadily and decisively forward. In any case I must stay here till the 16th August : for that date I already have the announcement of visitors from Germany (sister, friends, *et al.*).

You haven't made up your minds about the winter ? Am I really to renew the experience of how a winter is passed in Zurich without the house of Wesendonck ? I cannot get accustomed to it ; I should have to haunt the house itself, which I suppose you'll leave standing. You vagabonds : to build yourselves a house and run away from it ! Let me but have my house : I shall move in before the roof is on. God bless your dear self ! Best greetings from

Your R. W.

On the 7th August another letter came from Mornex :

Best Friend,

It is a real sorrow to me, that you cannot execute your trip to the Lake of Geneva until I have left it; for I thus am deprived of every chance of seeing you this summer.—Monday the 18th, I take the Lausanne post to Berne.—Liszt has definitely promised his arrival at Zurich for the 20th September. For the moment I am expecting an elder sister, also a Weimar friend who is making the journey expressly to visit me.—It pleases me much, to hear that you will be in such good company on your approaching mountain-tour, as that of Herr Zeugherr.[1] He is a well-intentioned, most deeply refined and cultured man, whom I could wish as companion to many on the paths of life—if not precisely to yourself—as well as of the Oberland.

With regard to my house-redemption-project I can tell you nothing, as Härtels have still left me without a definite answer; which makes me fear that my ultimate demand may have been too high for them. In that case I should have alarmed you for nothing. *Valeat mundus!*—But don't relax your care about me, for I still have a terrible deal to do on this earth before I can go to my rest : "Tristan" has now been joined by a second subject, which so engrosses me that I should like to swallow down all work between, just to get to the execution of this newest plan.   It will be called, "die Sieger."   Adieu! A thousand greetings from

Your R. W.

[1] The architect who afterwards arranged the little house which Wesendonck placed at Wagner's disposal at Enge, near Zurich.

This was soon followed by a letter (dated Sunday evening, Mornex) inviting Wesendonck to meet him on Monday the 18th August at Berne. The meeting took place, and thereafter Wagner writes from Zurich (without date, but obviously within the last ten days of August) :

Best Friend,

Once more my warmest thanks for the friendly rendezvous in Berne, with which you gave me a great joy. Since my return to Zurich, I already have thoroughly recovered, and can trace the results of my cure more distinctly every day. I found my household, as you already knew, increased by a few ladies ; of whom one, my sister, is particularly agreeable to me. Beyond these, my Weimar Regierungsrath and red-hot enthusiast [Franz Müller] had arrived, bringing me news already hinted me by Liszt, of such a kind as to set my plans for a housely future once more staggering. The other experience I herewith convey to you through Breitkopf und Härtel's letter, from which you will gather that no reasonable human being desires to league himself with me when once he comes to reason. My laboriously built up hope, nay, well-nigh certainty, I have to regard as demolished again, and anew I must resign myself to the tortoise-march of my sluggish destiny. By an extraordinary coincidence, on the self-same day I heard through a most discrcet, and at present confidential, channel, that the Grand Duke of Weimar quite seriously intends to draw me to Weimar by hook or by crook, and—informed of my pressing need of a thoroughly quiet, undisturbed and refreshing place of sojourn—thinks of offering it to me at the Wartburg or one of his pleasure-castles. Now, if this solitary wish, which I absolutely am not to see fulfilled in Zurich and its environs, should finally decide me to abandon an asylum that has become almost unforegoably dear to me through the presence of few but irreplaceable friends—perhaps to enter obligations which, even if not expressly stipulated, must still be implied,—it would be a fresh proof what trifles (taken broadly) often determine, rule and domineer the life of an artist of my stamp.

Otherwise I have nothing worth telling to report to you ; here everything is as it was. Let me hear what you propose doing, and be ever assured that I remain with gratitude and friendship,

Your

Richard Wagner.

Smarting from a slight inflicted by some third party, Wagner writes to his friend on the 1st September 1856 :—

That's just the way with me, dearest Wesendonck ! Here you have back the letter of B. ; please give your dear wife my best thanks for her effort at intervention.

Once more I feel much and deeply humbled ; the thing nearest my heart is a rooted resignation, as all my endeavours seem quite foolish to me. Indeed I can testify that I ask nothing more from the world than a workshop, and untroubled leisure to labour therein : fortune and happiness I do not desire ; yet

what I want is just what I ought not to ask of the
world, as it can't be its business to favour such liftings
above it.   That I feel quite plainly :—why don't I
cease from unallowable pretensions ?—There I am,
wanting to create a work which the purchaser doesn't
even deem worth the cost of nourishing the author
while he writes it ! And that's the sum-total of all
the applause and renown I have won ! Can anything
be bitterer, and yet—as the world is established—
more just ?— The very people best calculated to
represent the world in a worldly sense towards the
artist, from of old have been the Princes, because of
their being raised above the meaner needs of life and
all necessity of their supplying. If one pries into all
these protections, however, one notices as much of
oppressive, wounding, spurious there, as anywhere
else ; and : *I* am the least fitted to hazard the very
happiest exception, as I do not care a rap for the
externals that seem to constitute the essence of the
thing.

Now *you* desire to replace both music-publisher
and prince *entre nous* to the best of ability ? My
God, were I in your place and could manage it, I
certainly would do the very same, for giving is more
blessed than receiving ; that is precisely my nature,
seeing that giving (in my fashion) has really robbed
me of all my strength. I scarcely thank you for
your offer, as I know for certain that the feeling of
being able to make it, must be a pleasure that rewards
itself far more than any uttered thanks could do.
Should it come to your being able to carry out your

purpose with me wholly, and if ever I am to play a rôle in the history of Art, you surely should also occupy no scanty place therein ; and to preserve this for you with all energy and outspokenness, would be for me a true contentment of the heart. Have you a fancy to lift us both so high ?

Meantime I feel weighed down with lead, and still am incapable of any soaring to fresh hope : all seems to me so impossible, that could help me to rest and wholly free my tortured spirit.   From a noisy, ticking, tapping, hammering and clanking house, I stare into the world outside ; and the more I try to fix my eye on a point where I might find quiet, the more alien and incongruous does the world display itself before my gaze.   I see nothing before me but a horribly busy wilderness of grinning faces, and if I spy out traits of sympathy, they are always joined with the shoulder-shrug of powerlessness.   Is a miracle about to shew me power and sympathy combined in *you* ?   It's too good to believe.   Let me look a little closer, to come to fair deliberation !— Adieu for to-day !   God knows what is becoming of

Your
Richard Wagner.

According to his marginal note on Wagner's letter, Herr Wesendonck replied on the 4th of the month ; he was answered by the master on the 10th (September) :

Best Friend,

You are a dear good creature, and believe me that I deeply recognise the exceptional nature of

your interest in me. I almost despair, however, of
its being possible to help me! My life is a sea of
contradictions, from which I can only hope to emerge
with my death. What have you not already done
to help me and give my spirit rest! yet ever and
again all turns out insufficient. Especial needs,
peculiar deferences that I have to observe in my
immediate household,[1] unexpected disturbances, and
so on, make it hard for me with all my efforts to
find a certain rule of conduct.

Coldly as I once left Dresden, could I now depart
from Zurich too, where I have shunned no exertion,
no sacrificial zeal, at last to recognise that, as erewhile
there, so all my sacrifices here have been quite fruitless, and not so much as procured me the satisfaction
of discovering in any single thing the traces of my
action. I feel it is time to break with this portion of
my past, and I would do it if I had not knit a bond
in this very place as *never before* in my life. This is
the bond of thanks and heartiest friendship to Your
house. Believe my love of truth, that I now am
saying no idle thing. The boundless indulgence and
untiring proofs of interest that you bestow on me—
considering the many points of difference in our
natures—must have a deeper ground of sympathy
than can be met with often in this life, or saving
most exceptionally. In this assurance please behold
the only reason of my hesitation what to do, and
toward which side I ought to cast my vote.

---

[1] An invalid wife : an artist whose creative work could not be always noise-
less ; of such is the daily tragedy of life.

My wishes and sighs go out toward total repose and retirement : to be sure of enjoying these in the immediate neighbourhood of a family so kind and dear to me as your own, of always finding shelter and sympathy for sorrow and joy in these most intimate relations, would be a happiness *no* other could replace !—But can I throw this whole burden of my existence on you, and must I not perceive, after repeated experiences of the great difficulty of my position, that the load would grow too heavy for you ? As a fact, to me it seems time to come to a clear decision on this point, and to think of at least a division of the burden. Only, where should I place its true centre of gravity ? At Weimar, or in my refuge with you ?— —

The master goes on to say that the advantageous dispositions of the Weimar Court seem favourable enough to his livelihood, but the simpler relation offered him by the hand of a friend would lie nearer to his heart. In his hesitation he even entertains the compromise of passing each winter at Weimar, each summer on the Lake of Zurich, though that would not suffice his actual wish. He is anxiously awaiting Wesendonck's return from Paris, and closes the letter as follows :

So then—to our next meeting ! *How* we shall depart from it : with light or heavy heart, must soon appear. However things may go—we shall not part, I hope ! A thousand greetings from
Your R. W.

From the middle of October to the latter part of

November 1856 Liszt had made his visit to Zurich, ending up with a concert conducted by himself and Wagner at St. Gallen (Nov. 23). Returned to Zurich, the master writes an account of all this to Wesendonck on Sunday the 30th November, and conveys to him the compliments of Liszt and his companions on the visit, the Princess Wittgenstein and her daughter. He speaks of the success of the concert, and continues thus :

Liszt's "Orpheus" deeply interested me ; it is one of the most beautiful, most perfect, nay, most incomparable tone-poems : the enjoyment of this work to me was great. The public liked his "Préludes" better, which had to be repeated. Liszt was made very happy by my unfeigned recognition of his works, and touchingly expressed his joy thereat. The "Eroica" was small delight to me : in my indicible exertions to drive a tired-out orchestra to the height I wanted, my own pleasure in the thing was done for. To tell the truth, I no longer have a fancy for conducting Beethovenian Symphonies : I have drained them to their last drop.[1]—To tell you something good again, after my painfully prolonged stay at St. Gallen, and after safely getting through a public dinner (which was meant well, for that matter, and at which I was made so much of, that—against my previous obstinate resistance—I myself at last was brought to speech), last Thursday evening I returned to my domestic rest (?), and to this day

---

[1] At Zurich from January 1850 to February 1855 the master had conducted twenty-three concerts of the local Musical Society, with a preponderance of Beethoven's Symphonies ; after that the Philharmonic series in London, with all but the earliest two of the Nine.

have not since left the house. To-morrow I think of resuming my broken work with a will !

As result of this latest visit of Liszt's, I may tell you that my friendship for him has been materially strengthened. The charming candour with which he finally owned that he had much needed me, to get initiated into the actual depths of my work, agreeably dispelled all the misgivings roused in me by several symptoms of a superficial reading, so that I was able satisfactorily to answer for myself the question how that superficiality had been possible.

For the rest, my intercourse with the two ladies, and particularly with the Princess, has made a favourable impression on me after all ; in view of the Princess's great kind-heartedness, I have been led to greater gentleness and government of my so very excitable temper, so that I now return to my solitude as from a school, with the feeling of having learnt something. And how much should I not have yet to learn, to conform a little to the claims I make upon myself after close introspection, and to shew myself worthy before myself of what I hold for good and noble in this life of grief and weakness? Never has it become clearer to me than now, what indulgence is needed by the very best of us, and how he, of all others, has to practise the highest goodness, not to become the greatest wretch !

Now please fulfil our joint petition for news of yourself and your dear wife's health.—With a hearty farewell I wish you all the best !

RICHARD WAGNER.

The following letter is simply dated " A glorious Sunday morning " ; in all probability it was written as a sort of postscript to the above, for a letter of Wagner's to Liszt of the 30th Nov. '56, speaks of his having just hung " the Madonna " over his writing-table :

Dearest,

Besides letter-writing I had assigned this lovely Sunday morning to preparation and self-collection for my work : so I was just stealing down into myself, when the Murillo arrived. Again you have made a famous selection ! This pure ascending being shall be a fair omen to me ! — Heinrich had to help hang it up at once ; a magic radiance rains upon me from the wall.

Best and warmest thanks ! You dear, good, faithful benefactors !

Your R. W.

A letter of the 22nd December 1856 contains the following :

Children, what a magnificent portfolio you have sent me : it's quite impossible to put the ill-bred Siegfried in it ! God knows what I must save it for. It would have been nicer, however, if you had bestowed yourselves on us for Christmas : on that point, alas ! you are utterly dumb, and the handsome present has almost made me mournful, as it seemed to tell me you would stop away a long time yet. May I be mistaken ! Or do you mean—as good Prussians—to leave us in the lurch in the coming calamity of war ? That would not be handsome !

For my part, I am left enough already ; I fear that everything will leave me soon, even my relish for work.   I can no longer attune myself to "Siegfried," and my musical feeling already wanders far beyond it, away to where my mood fits in : to the realm of sadness.   Everything appears to me right stale and superficial!   Of our "loneliness" now you can form no idea, and my health, too, is dull and leaden. Perhaps—as a political exile—I shall soon have to depart from here, apparently for France, unless the Grand Duke of Weimar comes to my aid before.[1] Yet that really doesn't much concern me!

My hearty thanks for the precious gift, and particularly for the continued love and sympathy which you bestow on me.

In perpetual devotion,

Your R. W.

A letter apparently of February 1857, and referring to Wesendonck's announcement of the successful purchase of a little property adjoining his villa on "the green hill" near Zurich, begins thus :

" *Des Vaters Stahl fügt sich wohl mir :*
ich selbst schweisse das Schwert! "—

Thus far had I got, and was just thinking out the motive that is to characterise the rapid turn of events, the beginning of the wondrous smithy work, when your letter interrupted me with the *private* news ; so you may judge how it stands with my work for

---

[1] By obtaining from the King of Saxony the artist's amnesty.

to-day. But I well may give up the "to-day" when
I see before me so long, so beautiful and work-
propitious a "to-morrow," for which I have to thank
the rarest friendship and most faithful sympathy!—
You know what you give me with this news : whatever else this life may lack, must be denied me ; I
feel that I can but renounce, and must ground the
unattainableness of the desirable on my own self, my
inmost nature.   When this consciousness gradually
dawned upon me, and I had to seek my only consolation and relief thenceforward in the pursuance of
my art without avoidable disturbance, all my desires
and wishes, so far as hinging on this world, took but
one form : to find untroubled rest and leisure for the
carrying out of my artistic plans.   You know how I
told you this foremost wish just five years back, and
defined it as the longing for a cosy, quiet country-
house with garden.   This seemed a thing that ought
to be attainable, and you offered me a hand in it
yourself.   But time since taught me how difficult
was even this, and I almost had to deem that wish
unreachable as well, albeit—driven ever back thereon
—I never could quite give it up.   You remember
that I took the news of the acquisition of the plot of
ground by the mad-doctor, so disastrous to yourselves
in particular, with great composure as regards myself ;
for I was so at home in that sort of thing, so used to
shipwreck.   Would you like to know how I *to-day*
received the—entirely unhoped-for—news of the success of your negotiations for this property ?—A deep,
deep peace invaded me ; down to the foundations of

my being I was seized by a grateful warmth, that did not rouse the least excitement. But all at once such a sunny brightness came before my eyes, that I saw the whole world transfigured and at rest, until a solemn tear dissolved this picture in a thousand marvellous refractions. Dearest, I have never experienced such a thing before! so *radically* furthering a power of friendship had never yet entered my life; and what I felt was not precisely joy about the gotten property, but the glorious warmth conferred on me by the feeling of your friendship, the consciousness of being *carried*, that suddenly removed each weight, each burden from me. O you dear good creatures! What shall I say to you? As if at a stroke of magic, everything around me is suddenly transformed: all hesitation is at end: I know where I belong now, where I may weave and fashion, where find support and comfort, strength and recreation, and henceforth I can look unscared on all the chance and change of my career as artist, my toils and my exertions; for I now know where to find rest and refreshment again: in the most literal of senses at the side, within the bosom of the most faithful, most affecting friendship and love. O children! You shall be contented with me—indeed you shall! For this life I belong to you, and my successes, eh! my cheerfulness and productivity shall rejoice myself, for I will cherish them and love them, to make of them a joy to you!

O it is fine! This has decided *much*, yes *much!* could I depict to you the wonderful deep peace that fills my mind to-day!—

Now arrange for me to see you soon ; I yearn for
it with all my heart, even if I did not live so isolated
here. Sensibly enough, war is no longer to be feared,
and I think I may now remain here under shelter
even in that event. I shall write you again.

A thousand greetings !

Your R. W.

At the end of April 1857 Wagner moved into the little
house " on the green hill," and dwelt there with Minna his
wife for a year and a half. In the late summer of 1858
Minna's health became worse, and she went to live in
Saxony for quiet's sake, whilst Richard went to Venice, and
later to Lucerne, for his work at *Tristan und Isolde.*

In the autumn of 1858 his friend had lost a thriving
boy, and Wagner wrote him from Venice the following
lines of sympathy :

Dear Wesendonck,

My last words to your wife were my blessing
on the rearing of your children !—Your news has
profoundly shocked me. Accept the brimming tears
of a friend as tribute of his love !—The children, too,
had become very dear to me. I shall sadly miss the
little Guido when I think of your house !

O heavens ! All is so earnest, so earnest ! There
is nothing for us, save to clothe this earnestness
with gentleness and softness : but let us not rebel
against it ! It is our exaltation, and will become our
salvation !

I am still under the first impression of your news.
How gladly would I fly at once to comfort you.

May my sincerest sympathy afford you the consolation that I am deeply suffering with you!

And so—above the early grave of the dear little fellow—thanks!—and a heartfelt farewell!

Your
RICHARD WAGNER.

From Lucerne came a letter on May 26, 1859:

Dearest Wesendonck,

To-day my long-awaited box came altogether unexpectedly from Venice, which has really put me in good humour, and confirmed my belief that everything agreeable is purely negative; had things followed the usual order with this box, it never would have appeared to me as something special, whereas the whole contents are now as if newly bestowed on me, and in particular my [musical] sketches, which I already had half given up for lost. Now I have a complete library in my salon. So I will take this recovery as a good sign, and hope that many another interrogative in my situation will soon be bearably cleared up as well.

From Germany I hear that there is no hurry for my works; in face of the grand Germanic war, one can scarcely expect folk to trouble much about such-like art-trifles; time enough for that after the war! Yet I could wish that the gentlemen in Italy would come to blows a little less punctiliously; for before the war has begun, it cannot well come to an end, and it doesn't quite suit me to wait over-long. My projected American alliance is therefore becoming doubly valuable to me.[1]   Meanwhile I drink mineral-water ; it was time to take some active measure against the more and more rebellious basic matters of my earthly shell.   For sake of my work I wished to put it off ; yet at last I had to intervene : and now hope smiles on me that, with consent obtained from the Lower House, I may effect free motion for the Upper House of my microcosmic private parliament.   At present I can only work as if to while away the time, for one can't compound with minerals for ever.

Don't delay in duly carrying out your Lucerne plan, to which I so look forward.   May " Pentecost, the lovely feast," soon come for all of us.   Fare you right well !   Greet big and little children in your house, and think as well as you are able of

Your R. W.

---

[1] An American manager had announced his intention of visiting Wagner to negotiate offers from the other side of the Atlantic.

DEPRIVED of all means of subsistence, in 1859 the master had been offered a friendly loan by Wesendonck. In a letter of August 24 Wagner declines it with thanks. On the 28th of August, however, he reports the rupture of negotiations with Breitkopf und Härtel, and proposes "to do a little *business*" with his friend. The latter is to buy the entire *Ring des Nibelungen* (yet to be completed), the author retaining nothing but the performing rights and renouncing all profit from the publication of the music. This contract—in which Wagner declared:

I have firmly determined to accept no more assistance but such as flows from my work itself; in fact for some time past I have not accepted the allowance from the Ritters, against the most touching opposition of my noble friends—

was accordingly settled between the two friends, and Wesendonck paid Wagner in instalments the whole agreed amount. It must not be supposed, however, that Wesendonck regarded the sums of money given to Wagner in the light of a loan to be repaid; merely to spare his friend's feelings, and to relieve him of all sense of indebtedness, did he consent to give the mutual compact the form set forth above.

In the autumn of the same year Wagner went to Paris,

and began his preparations for the concerts he conducted there in January 1860, which won him many a friend. He writes to Wesendonck from his lodgings, 4 Avenue Matignon, Champs Elysées, on the 17th September 1859:

My dear Friend,
    I ought to be back in "Inferno" now, with "Paradise" lying far behind me. But luckily I have only got so far, as yet, as to halt on the green sward by the forecourt of Hell (though not in company of sages!). The quarter of Paris in which I am staying is quite new to me as a place of abode; its respectable retiredness and pure air make me hope I shall hold out. I have a good prospect of getting a permanent dwelling, and as I really am resolved to make a longish stay in Paris under any circumstances, in order to prove once for all if it still can be of profit to me, to-day I have given orders for my furniture to be sent on. For that matter, it is quite indifferent to me where I live, if I can only feel tolerably at home within my four walls, to indulge my old relish for work again. At present I am keeping strict incognito. Yesterday was my first attempt at calling on a few acquaintances, and I found them all still à la campagne, even our excellent Kietz.[1] The Olliviers will be back in a few days.[2] As I have been fully occupied till now by questions of abode, it is lucky that other relations engage me but little: and I believe I shall be able to dispense with them altogether. Conse-

---

[1] Ernst Kietz, portrait-painter, a friend of Wagner's first Paris period, 1839-42; see *Letters to Uhlig*, etc.
[2] Emile Ollivier, subsequently Premier, had married a daughter of Liszt's.

quently I can tell you nothing eventful about myself to-day.   What I dream away to myself, however, would be no pleasure to you to hear.   So I simply turn my glances back once more, to bid you good children another Adieu.   The four bright days on your hospitable hill have had a fair significance for me : they live in me still : as pledges of a noble happiness, such as never can be given, but solely won. Let us hold it fast !—Many hearty greetings from
Your R. W.

The commencement of a second letter from Wagner's first quarters in Paris, of October 5, 1859, appears to refer to Wesendonck's agreement to the contract of sale in the *Nibelungen* matter :

Dear Friend,
Here comes the promised letter.   What shall I write you therein ?   How much you rejoiced me by your first letter to Paris?   That can only be said in a very few words — to a person like you. Everything that comes from you can only add to my emotion and friendly esteem.   Indeed it did not need your assurances of how you had followed me, and felt yourself involved in my development : who could measure the result of our intercourse, and remain in the smallest doubt about it ?   But it was handsome of you to say it to me.   Accept my thanks !—
Best of men, life is and remains an earnest thing. Whoso has had this brought quite plainly to his consciousness, has to win his zest and courage from something very different from life and its concerns.

Certainly no one can accuse me of a dogmatic attitude
or stand-offishness toward life : there is no rooted
bitterness or scorn in me, and I take without question
whatever presents itself, though I certainly have not
to seek for it. But—it always returns very soon to
the primary key : and—then I stay so foreign to the
world, that I often wonder how much longer the
game is to go on.

However, to the point !—Will you believe me,
when I tell you that I drag on here precisely as at
Lucerne ? Only, as yet I work at no fine task
besides, and have nothing to do but write a mass of
letters. Even at Venice I now and then believed
that, with attainment of a feeling of callousness
towards the world, I should some day gain the
possibility of letting the superficial whirligig of a large
city revolve around me. Now, however, I fancy I'm
—too tired for that !—

After explaining how impossible it has become for him to
accept various invitations in Paris, though issued by cultured
and agreeable people, Wagner goes on :

Ah ! friend, but the talking ! The hours of
useless talking ! Either indifferent conversation—
what's that to me ? Or heated monologue about
myself—what's that to others ? And I always to
bear the costs ! I no longer can squander in this
fashion : I really am too fatigued. The Parisian
climate at present makes me very nervous, and I
often feel too weak for promenading. It will only
be well with me again, when at last I see some fruits

E

of my squandering ;—and that is, when I *work* again !
—What confirms me still more in my resolve to
keep a strict retirement, is the possible prospect of
yet representing the " Tannhäuser " here.[1] If this is
to come to pass, I can engage in it only under *one*
condition, namely that I concern myself with nothing
but the work itself, and hold off every vestige of a
coterie to be nursed by me.   My first stipulation was,
that I should not have to make the smallest concession
on this point.   The undertaking itself seems possible
for the middle of January.   The translation remains
the chief difficulty ; so far as I can see, my young
aspirant to a Vaudeville success,[2] with whom I have
hitherto plagued myself, will not do at all.   Now, however, the best imaginable prospect has presented itself :
I will let you know as soon as I have a favourable
answer, and meanwhile merely tell you that *Roger* is
now contemplated as translator.—

But all this is going on behind the scenes.—
With everything else I am having a deal of trouble,
particularly with my excellent Devrient at Carlsruhe ;[3]
I perceive that he, as well, has sunk fairly deep at
last in the regular routine ; for all his signal qualities,
his nature always suffered from a streak of leather,
which now appears to have lost its last elasticity.
The answers the man sometimes makes me !   And
yet I have to be glad if I can hear anything at all, as

[1] At the Théâtre Lyrique, under Carvalho's management : this project fell
through.
[2] Rudolf Lindau ?—Roger was a celebrated French tenor ; see *Letters to
Uhlig*, etc.
[3] About a performance of *Tristan und Isolde* which never came off.

to-day has been the case for the first time since my
Paris journey. Quite certain I can by no means call
the thing there, and still await from the famous young
Grand Duke right speaking proofs of an energetic
will.—Hark you, dearest friend! The other day
you taunted your wife with harbouring the idea that
I should return to Germany under no other condition
than that of being fetched-in in triumph. Now let
me tell you in strict confidence that I really feel as if I
ought to wait for that in truth—though I would make
anyone a present of the triumph, and that right gladly!

The abode is hired, and in fact—as I was bound
to—for three years with prepayment of the last two
terms. A pleasantly situated and detached little
house, like this, offers me the *only* possibility of a
stay in Paris ; thus alone am I guaranteed against
neighbours' pianos, which rage in every house here
with incredible fury. There I think, however, I may
passably last out my three years, provided the Swiss
mountains and a visit to the "green hill" refresh me
every summer. Just now I am busy furnishing, and
longing much for homelike rest and possibility of
working—which always mean the same to me.

So I suppose my position in the world is pretty
much this : I have scarcely any more great chagrins
to expect, but still great cares. Quite lately I received another exhaustive medical report on the health
of my wife, which has much distressed me again.
Yet I may hope that the *mode of life* which I am
arranging here for her, as well, will prove of benefit
to her condition, for the simple reason that I shall be

able to keep her away from excess of company,[1] in which she always excites herself too much through over-talking ; God grant she may find a nice sensible, agreeable female companion. I have had to veto her visit to Carlsruhe for the Tristan performance, in advance : for such exciting times, as the doctor agrees, she absolutely is no longer fit. For the present she has still to undergo a grape-cure at Dresden.—So there you have a piece of trouble from me, lest you should think I am hovering in the clouds !—

But you make me anxious too, with your news of Karl's illness.[2] Only, I reassure myself sooner there, as I may assume with the greatest certainty that it is merely a passing child's-malady, which, with the care taken of your children, will be of no consequence. Yet I beg the mother to set my mind at rest as soon as possible. And greet them all right well and heartily from me ! Let us soon see the photograph, and be assured that—on the green hill stays my home !

Your R. W.

Wagner soon removed into his new abode, 16 Rue Newton, Champs Elysées, whence he sent the following letter on the 25th October 1859 :

My dear Friend,

It troubles me, that I have disquieted you about myself. What am I to do ? Can I be frank, with-

---

[1] In the house in the Rue Newton, where Minna joined her husband later on, the first floor was reserved for her, the ground floor for the master.
[2] Wesendonck's eldest boy.

out complaining? Or am I, where alone I gladly give myself without reserve, to practise a friendly deception? And if I did, should I be believed? Were I believed, however,—what bitterness for me to know myself then *quite alone!*—Silence?—How long could that benefit, without alarming? I think, and walk each day with you. Then I say to myself: 't were best for me to take the pains to choke the reason of my cry, to make myself insensible, to fight off worry. But how begin it?—That I am alive, is the ground of every cry; that I am thus; that my whole being and doing place me so entirely out of all relation with the actual world, and yet I have to keep on living in this world, in it to satisfy my needs, —this generates the constant reaction under which I continually, daily, hourly must suffer,—and nothing can lift me out of it.—With all my thoughts and schemes I stand, and remain, too far outside all present possibility! Lest I should abandon everything and quite despair, just rarely now and then a tiny smile is cast on me by my surrounding, which surprises me the more and produces the greater effect on me, as it comes so unexpectedly and from amid the coldest strangeness. I remain receptive to it, and hardly know whether to take it for a blessing or a misfortune: a blessing because it holds despair aloof, a misfortune because it always casts me back again into the old circuit. My adventure with the douanier was of this sort,[1] as once the Strassburg episode

---

[1] Edmond Roche, custom-house officer in Paris, subsequently joint-translator of the *Tannhäuser* text; see Glasenapp.

with the Tannhäuser-overture. But I have grown
accustomed to fix my eye no longer piercingly and
lastingly upon this smile : nothing earnest, nothing
decisive to be awaited from it ; it remains but just a
smile, and only meant to cheer me for a moment.
For that matter, for the pursuit and execution of the
plan of a performance of the " Tannhäuser " in Paris,
e.g., it would need so good and permanently good an
humour (just so as not to take things too heavily)
that—as I don't know how to get and keep that
humour—I can hardly seriously believe in the success
on which everything now seems to depend, and to
depend because I otherwise see absolutely nothing
else before me than fresh confusion, fresh upset of
my situation. This always mingles so despotically
and determinantly in all my relations to art, that I
really shall never enjoy life, either, for a month at a
stretch !—God knows, this Paris was not my choice !
I seized it with none but the certainty of a man who
has no choice. After the completion of Tristan—
when, as you will remember, I wanted to leave Lucerne
at once—my purpose (which—like all such phases of
life—I had viewed in nothing but a hazy, floating
distance) suddenly rose in sharpest line before my
eye, and I recognised myself as so ill-equipped for it
that—as I wrote you—I let my hands fall powerless
to my side, and could think of nothing but to cease
from every effort and wait in utter apathy for what
was to become of me. From this unbearable condition I turned at last to you ; you put your oar in
splendidly : so the thing was to go. And yet, my

friend, it does not go. The reckoning was made
without the host ; and the comfortable sense of
security, with which I sketched the plans for my support, is over. This migration, the removal and new
furnishing, tear all my calculations down, and the day
when I rented this little house, and prepaid the last
two terms—as demanded for security—has become
the outset of interminable cares for me ! You would
not wonder at it, and certainly must only recognise
my abstinence, were I to detail to you the endless
malheur into which I have fallen. Let that be for
another time ! For to-day merely this : that of late
I have had with true grief to see my plan for compassing my livelihood by our Nibelungen transaction,
until the time when a fresh and lasting fund should
have arisen from other takings to be set aside meanwhile,—totally shattered ; at least it has become quite
impossible with [the proceeds of] " Rheingold " and
" Walküre." Listen with self-command, and don't
be angry if I tell you that, in increasing anxiety about
my immediate future, I have had to look around for
sources of assistance that might flow from my other
works. I was already drawing Tristan into this calculation, when Tristan is suddenly struck totally out
for a length of time : its first performance altogether
impossible for the present ! Now, here the truly
torturing conflict between my art and my worldly
interest comes again into clear sight. Believe me that I
had already become so small-minded (when I perceived
the growing difficulties of my Paris establishment) as
to wish to hold by Carlsruhe even with the voiceless

female singer ! I know what pain so mangled a performance would have given me, and yet I could almost
regret being freed from that pain. How do you
imagine that I feel in such a dilemma ?—So the Tristan
doesn't exist for me now : or— ?, but no ! that is
not to be even thought of ! At Berlin my Lohengrin
has lost his voice, and I look forward to a long pause
in the performance of that opera there.—So I must
turn my eyes all the more eagerly to the Paris Tannhäuser. Well, that will probably come off, and if I
have the humour for it, this outlook (which by all
means has its signal value for my situation) is assured
me. But it isn't to be thought of so all at once.
The Director is ready, and wants to be able to give
the opera. But how long they will leave his theatre
standing (as it is to be pulled down on account of a
new thoroughfare), he doesn't know for certain : possibly it will be demolished this coming March. On
the other hand they will build him a grand new
theatre ; I believe Carvalho wants to put Tannhauser
off till then. For a man who can wait, the affair
doesn't look so bad : but to be in my position with
it all, is—ignominious. However, I am getting on
with the translation. Roger will do the thing very
well ; without standing at the height of culture and
endowment to do justice to the poetic aspect of the
task, in everything else he is quite well fitted for the
translation. Only last Sunday did our *rendez-vous*
take place in his *Château de la Lande.* In the first
glow he had already translated the opening scene :
with my constant preparedness for evil, I was agree-

ably surprised this time ; he sang the scene himself right well, and the French text was quite singable, the accent correct, the phrase not markedly distorted. So I plucked up hope. He invited me to come out often to his country-seat, to work together there without disturbance. Yesterday accordingly I went again : I then perceived that I have to do with an amiable and gifted nature, which cannot, however, bear mental exertion for long, and willingly turns back to trivial habit. He had worked very little, and begged me to come oftener, to spur him on ; all the same he seized the first pretence to steal away from the pianoforte to the domino-table, where he stuck in bliss till I made my bow—in view of the hopeless company—and started back to Paris. Next Monday I am to go again. A terrible ill-humour, a wounded pride, often boils up in me : I seem to myself a wretch, degraded and unworthy of my being. God knows if I am understood ! What should I do, make, or effect ? Yet—I see well enough that I must try to find myself in Roger too : and he really is quite a charming fellow. His pretty talent has also blessed him : his property and goods are valued at a million [francs], and he has a castle too, in a great big park with lofty, glorious trees, to play dominos in. Then I come back home, and question if I shall be blamed for ordering *chênes* [logs] for all the hearths in my house. So wags the world—and if I'm in good humour, the Tannhäuser shall wag too. But—humour is needed for it ! That you see.

I regard this Paris project, when taken seriously,

as nothing but another of the tricks to keep on dangling something before me, to entice me to hold out. I know them! Just so am I now shewn a brand-new allurement for the "Tristan": the Dresden Intendant sends me word that he hopes to obtain the King of Saxony's command for me to come to Dresden for a first representation of "Tristan." But that could not take place before July next year. At least I should have singers with good voices there. Now what is one to say to it?

O children! What a mass of wretched stuff I've been writing you again! Perhaps silence would have been better. Yet this is the only language in which I can convey to human understanding what certainly is often not understood when I simply express my yearning for the *end*. All that I suffer, I bear through nothing but the power of the wish to have peace and security round me once more in this world of robbers, to be able—forgetting all my misery—to set to work again! Believe me, I no longer have a wish save this. Of late I have again come to the lively conviction that I can renounce even the performance of "Tristan," and everything, only to know that I may work on undisturbed! Now I am bracing myself, to get air again for my last act of "Siegfried": breathe I but that once more, then everything is alike to me. For this I see: I am entirely what I am, only when I am *creating*. The actual performance of my works belongs to a more settled time, to a time which I must first prepare for by my sufferings!

My most congenial art-friends have nothing beyond astonishment for my new works ; every one, who stands at all near to our public art-life, feels too feeble for hope. There I meet nothing save pity and sadness ! And they really are right ! Nothing teaches me better, how terribly I have overleapt all around me, than a good sharp look—down from myself—on those who stand between me and just that world.—

So let me work myself completely out : oh, had I nothing, nothing else to do upon this earth ! Rest ! Rest ! that the inner torch may burn soft and bright, which flickers so wildly under the breath of this life of want, and—soon must be extinct. Let me but create the works I there was given, in peaceful glorious Switzerland, there with my gaze upon the lofty gold - wreathed mountains : they're wonder-works, and nowhere else could I have received them. Let me finish them : then am I done with and redeemed ! But ask nothing, nothing else from me, and don't rejoice when " successes " beckon me : their price is fearful.—

A thousand greetings ! My heart is lightened : may your own not have become too heavy !

Your
RICHARD WAGNER.

On the 29th November 1859 the master wrote the following letter to Frau Wesendonck, which must be considered as partly addressed to her husband :

What great joy you have given me again, dear

lady! Believe me, if I had to recognise myself in none but the mirror shewn me by the world and all my friends therein, I soon should have to turn away with dread of looking back. Nor can I be quite open and true with any of them; there always remain spots and blind places, which I know not how to fill up. But if You answer me for once, how splendid I then appear; everything, including myself, then seems to me noble: I know that I am safe.—

Children, that we are *three*, is something wonderfully grand. It is unparalleled, my and your greatest triumph! We stand inconceivably high above mankind, inconceivably high! The noblest must become some day the truth: and the true is so incomprehensible, because it is so purely for itself. Let us revel in this high delight: it has no uses, and is here for naught—it can but be enjoyed, and but by those who are it to themselves.—

So be you welcome[1] on French soil: here the poet of the Nibelungen steps forth to meet you, and reaches you his hand. I congratulate you warmly on your journey to Italy. You go to find a boon that I am not to taste, and which I therefore wish you doubly. Enjoy the balmy sky, poetic land, the living past, for me as well, and thereby be you twice rejoiced. Gladly, beyond belief, would I be with you!—

R. W.

On the 12th December 1859, Wagner wrote to Wesendonck:

---

[1] "You" standing figuratively for "your letter," of course.

Dear Friend,

That I can write to Rome to you, to-day, is really very fine. I am all eagerness to know how the horrible sea-passage was got over, and though I need have no anxiety about your wife—who has gone through long sea-voyages so well ere now—I hope with all my heart that the children may not have suffered too much from it : we had many storms about that time, and even the Mediterranean may not have been exactly pleasant. But I soon may hope for tranquillising news, and assume that you are not waiting for mine before writing me, as you may guess pretty well that—in spite of Paris—I have not much to report.

In fact I will tell you nothing to-day about my Paris undertakings : everything still hangs in the balance, and anything of importance can only be decided later on.—

The firm of B. Schott's Sons at Mainz had addressed itself to Wagner, with the desire to publish the music of one of his dramatic works. The master accordingly asks his friend whether he agrees to his offering *Das Rheingold* to that firm in return for payment of at least the sum arranged between the two of them before. He then continues :

God knows what, and how things will go with me yet. On the whole I have very bad language for my German fatherland just now : the speechless cowardice of my friends, especially in the Tristan matter—about which one in particular [E. Devrient] once made such a mouthful, proclaiming my return *with* the finished

new score beyond all fail—has really something enter-
taining for me.   There all of a sudden a cautiousness
reigns, the silence whereof is quite charming.   Yet
my successes on this marvellous terrain must be very
considerable, that people at last should seek me out
as Schott's Sons have done : it really seems as if one
no longer could get along without me.

Here I find myself once more in the ever-youthful
function of a débutant.   After playing this rôle for a
good long time in Germany, and leaving there when
I was beginning to get a grip of the repertoire, I had
to go through the very same thing at Zurich, *i.e.* to
try and give people a preliminary idea about myself by
all the difficult expedients of a man who hasn't the
right means of execution at disposal, and must fall
back on his manuscript works.   Well, having at last
been installed there in my proper line by aid of
excellent stage-ventures, I start the thing afresh in
Paris ; I always remain the beginner, who first has to
make himself known.   Presumably that's the reason
of my still seeming so young to myself : age, with
its fruits, absolutely declines to set in !—Thus much
I see, however : I shall have to stick to it this time,
and if ever I am to think of the realisation of my
"Nibelungen," it can only be on the basis of Paris
successes.   Whether that work and the "Tristan"
will ever be performed, troubles no man in Germany,
and least of all my nearer friends.—As to what stands
before me in Paris, well ! about that next time.—

For to-day, however, don't be cross with me for
falling upon you in holy Rome with such uncanny

rubbish. When one writes to folk in Rome, one ought to have the decency to talk of something better than I've just done. However, I hope your first reports will set me also in the proper swing to find the sanctity to send you seemly greetings. My man, who was in service at the Pope's in Rome, tells me much about it all, and is burning for me to take him on a trip there: according to him, it's very grand. What do *you* say? But say it soon!—And now a thousand greetings and wishes from

Your

RICHARD WAGNER.

After the three Paris concerts, which cost him enormous expense and bodily exertion, Wagner writes on the 12th February 1860:

My dear Friend,

As yet I find no rest, nor—alas! any desirable matter to write you! I am this moment waiting for an acquaintance who, as stylist, is to help me with a few necessary French documents: while awaiting his arrival, I follow the dictates of my heart to send you at least another brief account of myself. I should have had no time at liberty for it, except in sleepless nights—several times over, in fact, I did make a beginning then, but recoiled in horror from the thought of forwarding such nightmares to you.

Now that I have plunged into the forlorn attempt to procure myself the means for the performance of my new works through Parisian successes, let it not surprise you to hear nothing joyful from me any

more.   You know me enough, that on this path no
joy can bloom for me : I do not seek applause and
triumph ; all I seek is the opportunity of disclosing
my new works—to few—but distinctly—that I may
die at peace. To this, applause and storms of approval
can only help me when accompanied by quite positive
results. To ensure myself these latter, now that my
three concerts are over, is my instant care. You may
imagine what a recreation this affords me, after the
untold strain of those concerts ! Let me hint to you
what cares those concerts themselves have left behind
them, since no trusty friend like yourself was at my
side : how the material difficulties and disappoint-
ments, which had to be carefully concealed from all
the world, exceeded every calculation. Let me tell
you further, that one main object of those concerts,
the inducing of a certain gentleman [in Paris] to
guarantee my German Operatic enterprise, has not
ensued, and I am just about to cancel that undertaking — so important for my whole immediate
existence (as it was to have secured me the first performance of "Tristan")—to write off my German
singers, who had accepted with enthusiasm, and thus
to leave the gist of my intentions entirely unfulfilled
—for God knows how long : and then you may con-
clude whether the enthusiastic acclamations, of the
Paris public could delight me.—As said, I am about
to make straight for the acceptance of "Tannhäuser"
by the Grand Opéra. Fould, the unfettered monarch
of the Grand Opéra, and Meyerbeer's intimate friend,
evades me : I must try to compel him through the

Emperor himself, whose—procurer he is, however!
Think of me involved in these labours of mine ; consider my character, and what alone I seek ; imagine what pretexts I need, what paths I must take,—and tell yourselves how I must feel!—

I have been interrupted, and now have merely time to hunt for a hasty close to these sorry lines! Whence, from the endless store of what I might say, should I pick in a hurry the thing most worth saying? Let it abide by the principal wish, that these few words may find you dear creatures in good health and high enjoyment of the beauties Rome offers you. I almost feel as if I could add nothing better to that wish, than that you—how shall I say it?—might henceforth forget me : you are too sympathetic, for the thought of myself, and what I now am plying, not to fill you with pain. And yet—oblivion? Is't possible? At anyrate invest your memory of me in the beautiful impressions you receive from Rome around you ; think of the time that once shall put an end to my unrest, and clothe it in the noble garment which now is cast on Rome beneath your eyes! Above all, guard your health : I also promise you to do my best to care for mine! But rejoice me soon with a report ; I know nothing about you since long. Let us hope that Rome's beauty and noble calm are to blame for it!

A thousand, and another thousand faithful, hearty greetings!

Your
RICHARD WAGNER.

F

A letter left Paris on June 5, 1860 :

Best Friend,

This day—on which, according to directions, I
should be able to catch you with my news again—has
come upon me without my having really re-attained
the mood in which alone I should always like to write
you.   I had wonderfully fine weather for my birthday,
and was so cheered up by it that I was able to write
to your wife in the best, the calmest of spirits next
morning, to thank her for your greeting.   So please
tell your wife that I haven't thought fit to add a
word to those merry lines, that the weather has turned
bad again, and Jupiter appeared no more.

And now a little to the friend himself!—Believe
me, it was through neither disinclination nor negli-
gence, that I left your last letter unanswered : I
wanted something fine and good to write you.   You
had heard the music in the Sixtine chapel with unmis-
takably profound emotion, and that woke many a
slumbering memory in me.—Yet I perceive that what
I do not carry out *at once*, I can't hold fast, and only
very artificially retrieve.   Now, however, I am living
in a period when true artistic self-collection becomes
ever stranger to me, without my having reached
instead a really practical view of life.   Not yet can I
desist from higher aims ; possibilities still hover round
me, such as the performance of my latest works ; and
I still am hindered from becoming practical master
of my nearest obstacles in life because I always walk
with eyes on distance, averted from the street and

road, and consequently have to stumble sorely over wayside stocks and stones. Thus I never arrive at a state of strict decision :—scold me, who will—but I confess that I haven't yet made up my mind as to which of my affairs I ought to treat most seriously. My innermost artistic interest is urging me to a speedy representation of "Tristan"; to the plan for the performance of "Tannhäuser" in Paris, artistically so indifferent to me, I am driven by the dislike of submitting myself to my German relations. Everything is shaping well for this plan ; it will be taken seriously, and everything is placed at my disposal ; the management sets great hopes on it ; between the Emperor and Princess Metternich it has become a matter of courtesy. It consequently is going, and takes care of itself; not a step has it cost me ; the thing has been arranged almost wholly behind my back. Yet I naturally remain cold and uneager about the undertaking. For me it is nothing else than a question of power : though the tantièmes of the Opéra in themselves are no such great profit, the Paris success must in all probability have important results, as a rapid spread over the larger provincial theatres of France and Belgium, and even adoption by the first Italian theatres (in London and so on), will be the consequence. What I might gain if, without any further efforts on this terrain, I could draw from it alone sufficient means of support for the rest of my life, to me is of the most decisive moment. For I *then* could deal with my newer works in the only way befitting them. I find myself in quite a flagrant conflict with my conscience, if I have to represent these newer works of mine to anyone as suited for an easy circulation. These works are so difficult and so completely remote from all current theatric routine, that my only hope of protecting them from total misunderstanding is to allow at least the first performances to take place under none but quite exceptional circumstances, and consequently to wait for opportunities such as are reserved for none but a man who has no need to think of time and money.—Well, it seems that my fate will lead me that way. A great, unusual success stands in prospect, almost past a doubt!

On the contrary, *everything is barred and bolted* that looks like a prospect of performing the "Tristan"! The Saxon ambassador to France, a very good man, is in Dresden at this moment, and there will personally endeavour to arrange my affair with the King. As yet I can scarcely believe in his success! Were that to arrive, however, and Germany to be shortly re-opened to me, I should know no theatre which combined the forces requisite for just my work. At Berlin the lack amounts to nothing less than everything. Vienna is in utter decadence ; and Dresden itself, which still might offer me the fittest company, must probably stay closed against my so indispensable personal co-operation for the present.

Now you may judge my inner feelings : *here* the "Tannhäuser," leaving me cold and uninterested, but thrust upon me under the most favourable aspects ; *there* the work that actively engrosses me, has need of me alone, but everything opposed to it! And I am to determine *freely* ? Yes, there are children who, in spite of thorough schooling, still prattle gladly of the human individual's *free will*. Should you happen to find such a one in your neighbourhood, just ask it about how the free-will should behave here ? Or whether, on the other hand, the naïve proverb " Man proposes, God disposes " does not contain a very weighty truth ? Perhaps this : Man wills, but God wills still more, and takes possession of the human will to will through it what does not profit it (the individual), but him (the God). As to the " God " we then might come to terms some other time, and probably find in the long run that there is no such mighty difference between the Individual and the God, especially when the former is possessed by God, *i.e.* has been placed in the position to do something out of the ordinary, something seldom successful and for the good of all.—But enough of exaltation, in which, however, I feel myself less proud than suffering !—

So for the nonce I am riveted to Paris, where it goes with me meanwhile as dolefully as possible. Just to *mock* my situation duly, within the last few days I was set the following trial. A Russian General, director of the Imperial theatre, came here and laid these two alternatives before me : either to go to Petersburg next September, remain there all the winter, produce my " Tannhäuser," conduct grand concerts, be guaranteed 50,000 fr. for it, and receive the half at once in cash : or nothing at all !—Each combination proposed by me, to fit in with the performance arranged for the same time here, was declared impossible. To next year my General would have nothing to say. Everything reposed on the jealous, but well-meaning plan of a Russian friend, who wants to carry me off from Paris to St. Petersburg, and hates Paris! —Well, friend : this time the free will spoke a word for itself ; so purely and entirely for money I could not sell myself. I remained true to Paris, shouldered the untold misery of my Parisian existence down to the period of the performances of my opera (of drawing the smallest profit from which I cannot even dream now, without annulling every favourable omen), and journeyed back to my Newton-street. Now, this street is soon to be sunk $3\frac{1}{2}$ metres deeper, to bring it to a level with the Boulevard piercing it. This ghastly circumstance affords me the opportunity of relieving my present position by cancelling my lease, which must be granted me, in fact, with a little compensation. From next October I shall therefore rent a smaller lodging in town, much nearer to the Opéra, at like time abandoning all idea of peace and comfort, as I really shall have to bid goodbye to the *Muse* for a good long while. When I established myself in this last little house I had absolutely nothing else in mind, with Paris too, than to resume my work soon, and be able to live in peace and quiet for it. Only when I mean to call and bind the *Muse*, however, do I seriously think of furnishing my house with rest and snugness : when I give her up, all that sort of thing has no longer any sense for me. If I have to do business, to fag myself out and come home half dead, then the narrowest nook suffices to give me rest. For this rest is something far inferior to the rest for creating. As I am not working at present, everything that looks like needlessness oppresses me ; and if ever I give up all hope of meeting the Muse again, some people will be astonished how little I need in that other rest !—

And now, what glorious copper-plates have come into my house ![1] Ah, children—what bitter tears run down my cheeks at times! Yes, I too, believe me! I too have yearned for the rest of a noble enjoying—: yet that will ne'er be granted me! Rest for creating, or rest for dying : in this sense alone, I know it, is rest allowed me. Yet how good, that the Noble really supplements itself : what I cannot, that should ye ; and what ye taste ye taste for me, and in you I too enjoy it. This rest is the best activity bestowed on you. So win it wholly, my beloved friend, and grapple it to your heart : open wide your brow, and through the noble things that you behold and taste, reach out an undimmed hand to me !

Thus I greet these splendid pictures : in my eyes they are the graceful shadow-outline of the sunny joy you have received : by them you prove to me the noble, world-dissevered happiness that Rome has given you both. How thankfully I take the thoughtful gift !—And now farewell for to-day ! Greet the wife and children. May you all, refreshed and well,

---

[1] Raphael Morghen's engravings after the "stanze" of Raphael.

have re-trod Cisalpine soil by now.   Ever with loyal thanks

Your

RICHARD WAGNER.

It will be remembered that Wesendonck had bought from the master the four parts of the tetralogy, present and future.   By the spring of 1860 Wagner had already been paid the stipulated moneys for the first three sections.   This will explain the following letter of June 17, 1860, from Paris :

My Friend,

I send you herewith an acknowledgment. that I received the money all right.—Since the rupture of my Petersburg negotiations I no longer can withhold from you the information that it was yourself, without knowing it, who helped me out of the terrible fix into which I was brought by my three Parisian concerts.   Just when it had become necessary to provide at once the costs of those concerts, which eventually ran to over 11,000 francs,—just when other hopes which had been inspired in me, of immediate reimbursement for those concerts, were totally destroyed, and everything was strained to the uttermost,—I had an answer from the music-publishers who had approached me about the "Rheingold"; quite unexpectedly they complied with my conditions, and sent me the demanded fee forthwith in a bill of exchange on Paris.

At like time I was written to from Petersburg, that the Director of the Imperial theatre would be coming

to Paris soon, to try to secure me for Petersburg
next winter on most advantageous terms.—You were
a long way off, and my case was desperate : the
concerts, once announced, *had* to be gone on with.—
I employed the Rheingold fee, in the presumption
that I could repay you at once from the profits of
the promised Petersburg engagement : then, too,
should you be told of what had happened.

Now this prospect, also, has recently been closed
to me. So I can delay no longer in acquainting you.
Every possibility of recouping you by other means,
I must disown as illusory. Nothing remains for me,
but to give you a receipt for the amount stipulated
between us for the last piece of the Nibelungen, and
ask you to consider the sum for the Rheingold as
thus paid back to you. I certainly shall execute the
last piece yet ; if that were not reserved for me, I
know not what could hold me still to life, when I
daily long for death with all my heart.

It is very possible that you will have reproaches to
make me ; impossible, however, that you will not
save them for a later period, when they no longer
might serve to increase the greatest bitterness a man
can feel toward life.—As to the precise arrangements
for publication of the "Rheingold," another time.
—Farewell, and arrive safely back at the green
hill !—

Your R. W.

On the 23rd August 1860 Wagner writes :

Best Friend,

— — In a week the rehearsals are to begin
for Tannhäuser, which is to be out by the middle of
September at latest.   I still am not quite ready with
the French score: I want to recast one scene entirely
(between Venus and Tannhäuser) and compose the
Venusberg ballet-scene all over afresh, but cannot
arrive at freeing my head from other businesses as yet.
Last week I took a few days' trip to the Rhine, to
wait on the Princess of Prussia at Baden-Baden, at
the instigation of the embassy, with which I complied
the more readily as I believed that a personal interview
would best convince me whether I might count on
this lady's intelligent assistance for my future German
undertakings.   She made a good impression on me,
expressed herself with animation and insight, and
assured me with much warmth of her adherence.
But I had received such disheartening accounts of
the state of the Berlin Opera quite shortly before,
that I didn't feel disposed to go closer, with the
Princess, into the details of a performance of my new
works at Berlin.   The very rapidly-determined trip
had this advantage, that it gave me the opportunity
of seeing the Rhine for the first time.   I went by
steamboat from Mannheim to Cologne, and was
astonished at myself for being so stimulated by the
interesting journey,—which I should have scarcely
expected at my time of life.   The Drachenfels
distinctly carried off the palm, with me: it gave the
trip a splendid ending.   It amused me to find that I
was expected at the same time in Wiesbaden, to

perform my operas there at once: all the world took
it for earnest, as I heard! My God, no! I can wait
a little longer now, and am really not in such a
hurry to meddle with the German operatic mess. I
never went near Wiesbaden, and propose in future to
go very little near anywhere else. Of emotion at re-
treading German soil—alas!—I did not trace the
faintest spark : God knows, I must have grown very
cold!

I thank your wife most warmly for her description of the rich accession to your picture-gallery.—
Now don't be cross with me for bringing these hasty
lines to a close, and merely take them as a witness
that even in the thick of business, and the most
abominable humour, I do not cease to think of
you.

Hearty greetings from your
RICHARD WAGNER.

Between this letter and the next, Wagner had been
obliged to move out of his little house, for reasons stated in
that of June the fifth.—Incidentally it may be mentioned
that he began an action-at-law to recover the two years' rent
paid down in advance, but appears to have failed in his
endeavour.—His next letter is written from his new apart-
ments in the Rue d'Aumale, October 20, 1860 :

My dear Friend,
    So soon as I have news from you, I am
always eased ; and if I've no particular cause for
writing, I then give way to the rush of occupation
and the pressure of my mostly evil humour, both of

which withhold me from sending you a letter. But
when you are silent I grow uneasy, and write to you,
not because I have anything good or important to
tell you, but merely to hear why you are torturing
me by silence! Let that be said to you quite
candidly! On the 1st October I wrote to your wife;
I am very disturbed at having had no news since
then, as I hoped at least to find a welcome on my
entry into my new abode, as announced.—Only
believe me, children, that my home is *with you*, that
I am in a strange land here, and only feel homelike
when I know myself safe on the "green hill"!
Forgive me, too, my niggard writing in this latter
time! Believe me, I am going through a quite unheard-of life; I cannot willingly decide on quite
brief lines. So I will simply give you a review of my
last few weeks.—After completing a literary work,[1]
whose publication, printing and correcting (not count-
ing translation) occasioned endless cares and petti-
fogging, I had to gird up all my powers to compose
a whole long, most difficult scene of "Tannhäuser"
entirely afresh; here, between annoyances with my
landlord and lawyer, troubles of the most vexatious
sort; finally a removal, at which I was the only one
on my side who could speak French. I had got so
far with my scene, that I needed but two days to
finish it; yet I had to give in and let the removal
take place, as my former dwelling was already unin-

---

[1] The Four Opera-poems: *Holländer, Tannhäuser, Lohengrin,* and *Tristan,*
translated into French, with a preface on "The Music of the Future" (see *Prose
Works* III. 293 *et seq.*)

habitable. This meant an interruption of the most obnoxious kind, which robbed me of all sleep for nights.[1] At last—the day before yesterday—I have fought it down, and finished the scene. And to all this you may add *daily rehearsals* of Tannhäuser for the last four weeks!!—daily conferences with scene-painters, regisseur, costumier, etc.—Knowing the extreme earnestness I give to all my occupations, you may readily imagine how this wears me!—Well, I now am in the heart of town, in a comparatively quiet street, not very far from the Opera. Much is thus made lighter for me, and the lodging itself, not very roomy, is yet quite habitable again, and—the thing must go forward!—The principal aim of my present arrangements, is to get quickly through with as much as possible at once, and then be able to keep myself isolated in my cell. Since last night, too, sleep is coming back a little.—

Now—agreeable news! At the Opera my Tannhäuser is being studied with a zeal, an earnestness, an exactitude and carefulness, such as have ever been my unattainable ideal of such a study. A like punctiliousness, and minutest care bestowed on every detail, I have never found even distantly approached at any institute before : my German singer Niemann rubs his eyes, and admits that he has learnt his part for the first time here. Beyond the uncommon excellence of the whole arrangements at the Opera,

---

[1] See *Prose Works* VI. 117 : " A Paris workman, after my threatening him with Hell for breaking his promise, replied, ' *O monsieur, l'enfer est sur la terre.*' "

I have especially to praise the extraordinary personal fitness of the chief officials : above all, the *directeur du chant*, who practises the singers at the pianoforte, is quite inestimable. All the technique of rehearsal is managed with a matchless neatness and exactitude, the smallest inequalities in the text and so on are polished down to the last grain (the translator is always present), so that I have just nothing to do but breathe the right spirit into a *technically* perfect thing. I declare aloud, that *never* has it been so well for me, and certainly will never be so well again in Germany. The same applies to every detail of the preparations ; the scenery and all the *mise en scène* will fully reach the acme of my wish in this regard. —Moreover I find in each and every one so entirely good a will, so hitherto-unknown a diligence, that with such arrangements I am sure of overcoming the most fine-drawn difficulties, and consequently shall be giving my work in a *completeness* never even attempted by me yet.

Under such auspices I can advise you with a clear conscience, dear children, to come and see Tannhäuser in Paris this winter! It will be the most perfect thing, in the way of performances, I probably can ever offer you. I count with certainty and inward confidence on you for this affair ! They still say the performance will take place in December, yet it may easily be put off until January. You shall have preciser information—so soon as the date is settled !

So I close this hurried message with the unspeakably blessed feeling of being able to earn your dear presence by this instant labour of mine; and to this I will add nothing further, in answer to your last communications, than that everything you told me has touched me most profoundly.—Adieu! Adieu!!

Your
RICHARD WAGNER.

In November Wagner's huge exertions brought on a serious illness, which threatened to develop into brain-fever. On December 6 he begs his friend for help:

My Friend!

— — Through my illness the Tannhäuser has been postponed, after all: I have exhausted everything, and myself am exhausted to the last degree; that you will probably gather from my applying to you once more, whom I ought to spare for ever! Yet I am certain of being able to repay you the amount at Easter, and this somewhat lightens my step.—One thing, however, I beg above all: if it is inconvenient to you for the moment, or should compliance with my request put you in the least ill-humour, please ignore it altogether and don't say a word about it in your answer.

Since a week ago I am regaining heart; my powers begin to come back. It was a warning!— Fare well, and keep good courage in hard times, you too.

From my heart
Your
RICHARD WAGNER.

Wesendonck at once sent what was asked for, and Wagner thanks him in a letter of December 16:

Best Friend,
— — Indeed I have fairly recovered my old elasticity : unfortunately my exertions—resumed too impatiently—somewhat overpass the forces of a convalescent.   Where and when I am to repair myself, God only knows : for the present I am doing my best, at the doctor's orders, with all kinds of strengthening diet.   My employment is quite incredible ; but the worst of all is, that I still am very much behindhand with my composition work. The first dance-scene in the Venusberg isn't touched, and I've no idea as yet how I shall set it.   And then this absorbing Paris, in which, for all my keeping myself a hermit, I can't prevent folk bothering themselves to whom I don't exactly want to give offence.
      Through my weeks of illness a delay in the study of Tannhäuser has certainly occurred, yet I still reckon on the last week of January, that is to say if I can get my compositions ready in time, by a miracle.   We are now beginning the preliminaries for the actual *mise en scène* ; *i.e.* the finer shades and main dramatic situations are settled in a foyer furnished with a stage.   In this fashion the new scene between Venus and Tannhäuser has already been worked out ; it makes an extraordinary impression.   Both artists will be admirable.—Soon we shall be thinking of descending to the stage proper ; then

will come the orchestra too (as last thing), which
has hitherto been practising apart. My authority
remains unquestioned, in fact is stronger than ever,
as the Princess Metternich (who becomes more and
more attached to me) and Walewski, the Cabinet-
minister, are especially friendly. — So — as God
wills!—

Give my hearty greetings to your wife, and tell
her that I have spent a happy Sunday to-day,
namely wholly at work, without either going out or
receiving anybody!

And hearty greetings to yourself, dear friend!
Soon more!

Your

RICHARD WAGNER.

A letter from the period of the last rehearsals for *Tannhäuser*, therefore somewhere about January 1861 :

Best Friend,

A rascal gives more than he has; I
fancy I've just two minutes to dispose of, so they
shall bring you a laconic note.

Don't entertain the smallest doubt as to my
exerting myself superhumanly at present. Yesterday morning at $\frac{1}{2}$ past 2, after a night of vigil,
I finished the remainder of my new compositions for
"Tannhäuser"; the same day I found it necessary to
undertake a further alteration, in the Minstrels'
Tourney, for which I require a clear head. Rehearsals every morning, and 4 times a-week in the

evening.   Moreover—the old tale—each and every
accessory to attend to myself : at 11 o'clock this
morning a rehearsal with the horns for the hunting-
music ; impossible to get them anywhere in Paris,
but made possible at last through personal exertions
of the most inconceivable sort.   Atrocious lumbering
of a wagon with any number of wheels, but no
coachman !   I have to be everywhere ; for much,
nay all, is so unwonted to the people !   Special
practice, or personal drudgery (if you will), with
the singers, who are all beginning to feel how much
they have to learn over again from me.   Then a
growing rush of unavoidables !—My pulling through
—a perfect wonder !   The performance on 15th to
20th February.   If you can come yourself, it will
be a great delight to me !   I need something
pleasant—believe me there !

I have hopes of a fine, highly - finished performance, though not supplied throughout with
quite the most appropriate talents (non-extant !).
My alterations have turned out very notably, and
make the coming execution most interesting to
myself.—

I must be off for a *mise en scène* of the
Reception of the Guests at the Wartburg.   At 7
o'clock this evening a full orchestral rehearsal.
Before table, at 4 o'clock, a Concert-committee, to
which I must go to ensure Liszt's appearance in
Paris.   Adieu !   A thousand greetings !

Your R. W.

On February 8 the master writes :

Dear Friend,
        During the fat days of Carnival, when we
are unable to rehearse, I hope at last to gain a little
breathing-space to write a proper letter to your wife,
to whom I long have owed an answer.   Your lines
just received to-day bid me send you a brief note
forthwith.
        The first performance is definitively fixed for the
22nd February.   This really gives us ample time,
and only quite unforeseen mishaps could cause a
short postponement.—So come of good cheer, and
take it for granted that I would send you news
immediately, should a postponement occur.   If you
have reasons that make it desirable not to undertake the horrid journey in this inclement season of
the year, you may be sure of finding performances
enough to choose from in the kindlier Spring ; for
" Tannhäuser " will be played till at least the end of
May—Niemann's term of contract—probably with
scarcely a break.
        That you wanted to come so generously to my
aid at once, was worthy of a friend ; in my present
unparalleled strain I have not yet arrived at a clear
idea of my situation ; there's time enough for that,
and in case of need I will remember your friendly
offer.   At present I haven't a notion in this regard !
        Lately I paid the penalty for having accepted an
invitation to dinner as a great exception ; I was very
bad afterwards.   Only the fullest repose can at all

avail me after my exertions; in what these consist,
you probably will soon learn closer.   Enough for me
to tell you that a night slept through from 1 to 8
A.M. is an ideal happiness to me, which I only taste
as an utter rarity.—

And now a thousand hearty greetings! Frau
Mathilde is to expect a letter from the ingrate in the
jours gras.   Fare splendidly well!

Your

RICHARD WAGNER.

The Paris performances of *Tannhäuser* did not commence
until the middle of March 1861.   It is well known how
they were exposed to the most disgraceful treatment by a
fashionable clique of wreckers.   In consequence the author
himself put an end to them after the third (March 24) by
withdrawing the score.

As Wagner does not mention the performances themselves in his letters to Herr Wesendonck, we may here
adduce the report of an eye-witness, from Fräulein Malwida
von Meysenbug's *Memoirs of an Idealist*.   (The master's
own account of the episode will be found in Volume IV. of
the *Prose Works*, pages 347 *et seq*.)

" At the preliminary rehearsal "—writes Fräulein
von Meysenbug—" everything went magnificently;
and after the glorious Sextet, where the Minstrels
welcome Tannhäuser back, the orchestra rose as one
man and cheered Wagner in the gladdest enthusiasm.
It was 1 o'clock at night when the rehearsal ended.
Wagner was full of delight that the affair seemed to
promise so well, and challenged his wife to come and
sup at the Maison d'or in the Boulevard des Italiens.

We sat in a little private room.   It was a happy time,
that midnight hour succeeding the splendid rehearsal.
Wagner told us, among other things, how he had
explained the part of Elisabeth to young Marie Sachs
—whom he had chosen for sake of her beautiful
voice, although she was a novice—and in particular
the passage where she has to answer Wolfram's
question whether he may escort her, by dumb
gestures signifying : 'I thank thee for thy tender
friendship, but whither my path leads, none can
accompany.'

" Shortly after this fine rehearsal, however, the
prospects of success were troubled.   The imps of
mischief, always so glad to mar an ideal moment in
man's life, set to work to blow up clouds of envy,
grudge and hate on every hand.   The Claque,
formally engaged by every other composer, had been
positively banished by Wagner, and naturally foamed
with rage.   Then again the young Parisian lions, the
dandies of the Jockey Club, were angered that there
was to be no ballet of the usual form and at the
usual hour, i.e. in the second act.   What did these
fashionable rakes care for the performance of a chaste
work of art, which celebrates the victory of hallowed
love over the frenzy of the senses ?   Even before
hearing it, they were bound to hate it and condemn
it ; in effect, it was a sentence on their inner coarseness
and measureless depravity.   They armed themselves
in advance with dog-calls, through which to sound
their cultured verdict.   So the clouds were gathering
more and more threateningly, and it was with alarm

that I went to the dress-rehearsal, to which I took the little Olga [1] with me, as I wished her to learn a love of art from its greatest and finest examples. The rehearsal went off without outward disturbance. The numerous audience consisted for the most part of friends, among whom the Princess Metternich was conspicuous for her lively demonstrations of approval. To me it was a heavenly evening, for it brought me what I long had yearned for ; and though I felt that the performance left much to desire and would not satisfy Wagner, yet many a point was very fine, and at anyrate I now had an impression of the whole that confirmed my presentiment. On Olga, too, the charm had the effect I hoped ; she sat in rapt attention without ever getting tired, although it was quite late at night before the rehearsal ended. Upon going out I met Wagner, who was waiting for his wife. By the expression of his face I saw how little he was satisfied, and how little he expected from *this* production a triumph over hostile powers. A day of nervous waiting passed ; then came the first performance.

"I was in a box with Olga and some ladies of my acquaintance. The overture and first scene went by without disturbance, and though the management of the satyr-dance in the Venusberg fell far behind Wagner's idea, and the Graces appeared in pink ballet-skirts, it yet was good enough to make me breathe again and hope that our fears would be

[1] Frln. v. Meysenbug's pupil and daughter of Alexander Herzen, who at that time was living in London.

scattered. At the change of scene, however, the
wonderfully poetic transposition from the frenzied
Bacchanalia there below to the pure morning-stillness
of the Thuringian valley, as soon as the goatherd's
shawm was heard there suddenly leapt forth the long-
prepared attack ; violent whistling and hubbub quite
drowned the music. Naturally the opposite party
did not remain inactive, i.e. our friends and that
portion of the audience which wished to listen quietly
and then decide. As the latter were the more numerous, they held the field ; the performance went on,
the singers kept their heads and did their best.
Only, it was not long before the noise began again :
similarly the protest of the well-disposed, who always
had the better of it ; so that the performance arrived
at its proper ending. Yet it had been so cruelly
disturbed and hacked to pieces, that even the best-
intentioned had had no opportunity of forming a
right idea of the whole.

"On the following day I went to the Wagners.
I found *him* in a state of manly composure ; and so
much was this the case, that even the most furious
of the journals, in the battle which raged at once
in the press, acknowledged that he had behaved with
the utmost dignity under the tempest on the evening
of performance. From its commencement he had
determined to withdraw the score and make a further
representation impossible. We all — his nearest
friends—voted against such a course, as we hoped
for certain that the piece would win its way.

"So the second performance arrived. The hostile

party had arrayed itself still more decidedly;
equally so, that of our friends. The fight was even
more embittered than the first one. I was in a box
with Wagner's wife and a Hungarian lady. Next
to us were some Frenchmen who made themselves
particularly prominent by their whistling, hissing and
shouting. I was beside myself with indignation, and
gave my anger vent in French : '*This* is the public
that pretends to dictate to the world what is taste,
beauty, excellence ? It is a heap of street-urchins,
who haven't even manners enough to give other
people peace and time to listen.' To this effect I
spoke quite loud, so that Frau Wagner whispered
me in terror : 'My God, you're too daring ; you'll
draw unpleasantness upon yourself.' But I thought
of nothing save my wrath and scorn of such an
audience, and at last I turned directly to our neighbours, and said : 'Gentlemen, if you have regard for
nothing else, at least consider that the wife of the
composer is sitting next you.' For a moment they
were rebuffed, and became quieter, but then began
again. However, the opposition did not succeed in
bringing the curtain down, and the performance
reached its end once more.

"Wagner was now still more inclined to stop
further scandal, but all we others voted for the third
performance. It was to be given apart from all
'abonnement,' and we therefore reckoned that the
disturbers of the peace would stay away, making
place for the public who really wished to hear.
Wagner, however, had decided not to be present

this time, to spare himself the useless agitation ; the same with his wife. I had taken box seats for myself, Olga and the little Marie, who was staying with us. I hoped they would have an undisturbed enjoyment of this representation. Unfortunately it happened otherwise ! The rowdies had assembled in still greater force to continue their work, and appeared at the very *beginning*, against their custom. The singers behaved with truly heroic courage ; they often had to stop for a quarter of an hour at a stretch, to weather the storm that was raging in the audience. But there they stood, gazing fearlessly upon the public, and as soon as it was quiet they resumed their parts ; so that the performance was pursued to its end once again, though the maniacal din naturally spoilt all pleasure in individual achievements and fine scenic effects. The little Olga was as much excited as myself. She already had a great veneration for Wagner, and the depths of her young soul were stirred by this music, which formed her first real introduction to the realm of Tone. So marked and wonderful was its power over her, that I was convinced afresh of its inner truth. Olga took an impassioned part in the faction-fight, lent over the edge of the box, and, pointing to the gentry with the whistles, cried with all her might ' *à la porte, à la porte !* ' Two gentlemen who sat beside us in the box seemed quite delighted with the child's enthusiasm, and several times said ' *Elle est charmante !* '

"It was 2 o'clock at night when we accompanied a few friends to the Wagners, who would certainly be waiting up for a report. They were sitting cosily at tea, and he was smoking a pipe. He received the tale of the renewed and most remorseless fight with a smile, and joked with Olga, saying, 'I've heard you hissed me!' Yet by the trembling of the hand he reached to me I felt that the hideous fact had hurt him deeply. Though the whole atrocious coarseness and brutality of the incident recoiled on the public that had made itself guilty of such behaviour, it meant for him another hope gone, and the stony path of life lay once more gloomy, drear and comfortless before him! It cut my heart the more, as every effort to assist stayed fruitless. — Wagner now, of course, withdrew the score, and thus an end was put to the war at the theatre. In the press, and in society, it went on savagely for weeks. Since the time of Gluck its like had never been heard. There were very few voices that trounced the audience's behaviour, but they came from no unimportant quarter. Among others, the aged Jules Janin wrote a very sympathetic article. I sent a report of the occurrence to England, which was printed in the ' Daily News ' and shewn me with great delight by Klindworth on my return to England, without his knowing whence it came.

"Wagner travelled soon afterwards to Carlsruhe, in answer to a flattering summons from the Grand Duke of Baden. Thence he went to Vienna, where he heard *for the first time* a work long known to the German public, his *Lohengrin ;* he was delighted with the performance, as he wrote to his wife, who shewed me the letter. There he received the most enthusiastic ovations, which were really to be regarded as a *counter-demonstration* against the Paris treatment. I was rejoiced at hearing the good news, after he had gone through so much bitterness and horror."

Three months after Wagner's terrible disappointment in Paris, he wrote from that city on June 25 to Wesendonck:

How goes it with you, dear Friend? I know to what great cares you are exposed at present, and cannot think of you without anxiety, especially when I hear nothing from you. Let me have some news soon!

I now am passing through a most depressing time: my heart is so full of bitterness, that there's scarcely room for care itself. My whole life and work to me seem quite in vain and useless, and I appear to have spent too much earnestness on what the world, after all, but deems *a game*. In this time of trial, when each resolve is made impossible to me, whilst I am incapable of any mental activity, everything combines to give me still more pain! The day before yesterday the dear good little dog you once sent to my house died suddenly, and in an almost inexplicable fashion. I had become so used to the gentle creature, and the manner of its death, everything—has made me very sad. I know that you will not allow of attachment to dumb animals; but for a man like myself—and particularly in present circumstances—you will understand that this loss has been peculiarly keen.[1]

If I were only out of this Paris, where I experience nothing but misfortune! Towards the middle of next month I must try to manage it by force. How, where—else? Ah God, all is so highly indifferent to me. I have no roots anywhere, and each feeling of home becomes more and more foreign to me!—

How wrong it is of me, to bring my cries to you! Unfortunately I can bring forth nothing else, if I am to talk about myself. Nor did I want to do that, either, but only to know for certain how it goes with you. I know what cares are weighing on you, and, with my bent to sad forebodings, I fall on gloomy thoughts about them when I hear nothing ; for believe me that, if I have any feeling left of home, it goes out to where I felt myself in such safe keeping. So—nothing in answer to these lines, save the news of your welfare ! For that I beg you !

With heartiest greetings to your dear wife,
Your faithfully devoted,
RICHARD WAGNER.

---

[1] During his prolonged stay in Paris 20 years earlier, Wagner had had a favourite dog stolen from him ; see *Prose Works* VII. 63.

Towards the end of 1861, when Wagner made a visit from Vienna to his friends who then were staying in Venice, and discussed with them his gloomy prospects, Frau Wesendonck reminded him that he once had made her a present of the sketch (1845) for a comic opera, *Die Meistersinger von Nürnberg*. Comforted by the idea of devoting himself once more to his art, the master cried: "That *is* a thought! Send me on the manuscript at once to Paris."[1]—A month later the poem was finished, and soon thereafter in the hands of Frau Wesendonck.

In order to be able to continue his work at the *Meistersinger* in quietness, and at the same time be near to his publisher Schott of Mayence, Wagner put up at Bieberich on the Rhine in 1862. On the 21st July, after a disheartening interview with his publisher, he applied to Wesendonck to help him once more in his extremity of need, as he even lacked the money to provide his invalid wife with sufficient means for her removal to Dresden. Of interest to *us*, the letter contains only the following:

Of late I have had many visitors: the Bülows have been here for two months; for a time they have been joined by Schnorr of Carolsfeld (the son,

[1] The German says "Vienna," but in his letter to Frl. v. Meysenbug of March 12, 1862, Wagner speaks of having "shut himself up in Paris for four weeks, to write the Meistersinger poem. At the end of January it was finished." Evidently, therefore, the incident above-narrated must have occurred on one of his journeys back to Paris from Vienna, with a détour to Venice.—Tr.

tenor) with his wife, both of whom I am coaching in the " Tristan," which they hope to bring out at Dresden this winter.—The Meistersinger work is going well, but alas! so slowly that I still am much troubled about my immediate future.—

His friend helped him loyally, and Wagner wrote again on July 26 :

Dear Wesendonck,

The very resolve to turn to you for help had a tranquillising effect on my mood and situation, as I know from experience your undiminished patience—despite the sacrifices you have made me—and continuance in sympathy with my strange and everlasting worries.

Let me give you a brief report on the state of my work. When I took it up, I yielded to the hope of being able to finish it with all speed, so as to hand it to the theatres for the coming winter. In part, however, I was so engrossed by cares and troubles of every kind, that for a length of time I was absolutely incapable of production ; in part I soon learned so thoroughly to recognise my attitude towards my present works (which I cannot possibly throw off post-haste, but only find pleasure in when I owe their very smallest detail to good fancies, and work them out accordingly)—that I had to renounce all idea of such a scamped and sketchy work as alone would have been possible in so short a time !—And now : through you I've won fresh breathing-room and outlook ! On the Viennese performance of " Tristan," to take place in the late autumn, I don't count much ; yet I expect to have done a good half of my work by then. At present I am in the finale of the first act. Latterly I have been very much torn from the mood required for my work by the visit of the Schnorrs, who were here for a fortnight studying the " Tristan " with me with great success ; and just now I can do no more than instrument what I had ready.—But I shall soon collect my wits again, and — thanks to your fresh proof of friendship — am hoping for an energetic resumption of the work.

My friend ! The Grand Duchess of Baden believed she recognised a fond experience in my *Pogner*, which I read out with especial warmth, and her last words were the advice to choose a first-rate representative for this rôle in my distribution of the parts. I was quite peculiarly pleased by this impression. To myself, in the affection with which I have handled this part—now in the music too—it really is as if I had been setting up a monument to a friend !

God grant good tidings of your poor dear wife ! Else were all cheering and enlivening news in vain ! —May it all end well !

A thousand good, but sorely anxious greetings from   Your

RICHARD WAGNER.

Soon afterwards Wagner received the desired account of the recovery of Frau Wesendonck.—In September he begs again for help, which he is sure of being able to return later on, through the *Meistersinger* fees ; then follows his letter of September 29, 1862 :

Wesendonck! You are a unique man! Immediately after writing you last I suddenly grew cheerful and at ease—for the first time since this ghastly crisis. I seemed to be safe at once!—So that yesterday (even before a word from you) I was able to *work* again ; the first time for months !

Let me keep the " Walküre " a little longer : I am now entirely alone again, and need that sort of company at times !

You shall very soon have news,—and something else from me !—

Heartiest greetings to the wife, and sincerest thanks to yourself !   Your R. W.

On December 21, 1862, the master writes from Vienna : " I am saving myself as much as possible, to be able to get through the rehearsals, and my concert itself on the 26th." He then goes on :

— At the same time " Tristan " is being practised diligently.   In the second half of January *that*, too, may possibly be ready for performance.   The début affords me no good prospects : I am wretched and weary of life.   If I can get over this first concert, things will probably go farther : but I am not fit for much just now.

Don't be cross with me for the briefness of these lines : I am thoroughly exhausted and overworked !

Hearty greetings to the whole house and the green hill !   Your

RICHARD WAGNER.

King Ludwig II. of Bavaria had summoned Richard Wagner to Munich in the spring of 1864, and honoured alike himself and the artist by his intimate friendship. The two later groups of letters, however, will prove for how brief a time this happiness was accorded to the master by his enemies in the land. From this period, and in fact when the clouds of envy were beginning to gather thickly round him, dates the following letter of July 31, 1865:

Dear Wesendonck,

Though I arrive at little rest to resurvey my past with any clearness, it suffices to breathe to myself *your* name, to call one of the most important periods of my life so plainly back to mind that my heart at once is filled with the tenderest feeling of thanks for your kindness and friendship, and turns in friendliness towards you. How it was that your friendship, your willing sacrifices, yet brought me no repose, no peace, I must try and explain to myself: I understand it when I grow aware that no relation in the world, no friendship, no affection, could ever bring me peace and rest. I understand the past, in which you also were so nearly swallowed up, when I look back upon it from the extraordinary strain and turmoil of the present, wherein has been so strongly woven the most sincere and ardent love of a wonderfully - gifted Royal youth to the ripened, peace-desirous man.—Peace and rest have not been granted me :—that surely must have its own deep cause !—

Yet how happy, if I can find peace in remembrance at least ; let me dream of rest in thinking of the time when I lived beneath your shelter, and created ! It was a powerfully productive period ; even yet, with the greatest exertions, we haven't got so far as giving to the world what then was made. The disturbance that drove me from you, six years back, ought to have been avoided :[1] it made my life so foreign to me, that you yourself no longer recognised me when I returned to you at last for awhile. That grief should have been spared me too : to myself it seemed as if 't were possible, and beautiful would it have been, very beautiful, nay, sublime, had it indeed been spared me,—but one must not ask for the Sublime,—and I was wrong.

Now much has altered with me. Everything around me has become almost new. Yet this new world is animated by nothing but the effort to put new life into the old. The "Nibelungen," too, are to be resumed, finished, and set before the world. What your most generous and self - denying sympathy could not achieve, *none*

---

[1] See the preface to this volume.

but a King can now lead to its goal. I have confessed to you that, with my departure from your neighbourhood, my life slipped down a current that swallowed everything once reckoned for the furtherance of my creation. Even the rich advances which you made me on the publication of the Nibelungen works were engulfed in an outlay that stood in no helpful relation to those works. More than a year ago I had to beg you to view those advances as lost, since there was no possibility of regaining them by publication of the works themselves. I now may think myself lucky, even to see them published at all : for the " Walküre," a copy of which I send you to-day, I can get nothing from my publisher save a trifling set-off against the advances which he made me on the " Meistersinger," a work whose completion still lies very far from me. Yet, if I ask you now to give up all your claims upon my Nibelungen works, it is not that I abandon the hope of some day repaying you your advances themselves. Naturally this can be accomplished only through the generosity of my Kingly friend. But if I am to think of the liquidation of even such private debts by him, I necessarily must wait with patience for the favourable season, and beg you to wait also. You will understand how careful I must be for the moment, not to involve the youthful, scarcely adult benefactor in any too great system of expenditure for me. His consuming thought is for the performance of the works themselves ; we are founding a special school for training the performers, and a special theatre is to

be built for the festival representations. You have
had evidence enough, how plans like these inflame
on every hand, what menaces and persecutions these
projects of the youthful King have already drawn on
me. I know that you will be the first to admonish
me to prudence and moderation here, and—as that is
in your power—you of all others will certainly assist
me by your willing patience to exercise that prudence
and moderation. These works, however, both
should and must belong to the King of Bavaria.
Even "Tristan und Isolde" I shall allow to be
performed nowhere else,—and now, most likely, not
even in Munich itself. The "Nibelungen" can only
be given as a festival-gift by the King to the nation ;
with the ordinary Theatre, the gamble for likes
or dislikes, sale or non - sale, it is at end. Assuredly, dear friend, you will kindly understand
me, and not misconstrue my petition, if I
beseech you from my heart to grant to the fulfiller
and presenter of the Nibelungen - work the sole
possession of what therein is *my* work. Please
understand me, and be kind to me, when I beg you
to yield with a good grace to the King of Bavaria the
original score of the "Rheingold" now in your
keeping. The King shall and will hear of your
rights over this work : I feel sure that he will not
leave you unrewarded. If we now defer that recom-
pense, it is in reliance on the kindness of the old friend
who by this fresh proof of his noble sentiment will
contribute to the welfare of the creator of those
works himself in such a way that he gains rest and

leisure to complete and represent them. Surely you will not be angry with me, and understand my prayer?

How much I need benign and good experiences even now — ah! now of all times—I have not to assure you? What powers are master of my life, to rack my heart and scare me with the most unheard-of ills, you surely see without my needing to recount them to you. If under the grand impressions of the rehearsals for my "Tristan" I dreamt awhile of actual crowning of my long and grievous life as artist, I need but to remind you that a week ago I returned from the corpse of my noble, splendid singer,[1] to tell you what my thoughts must be about my fortune!!—

Many hearty greetings to your dear wife. She keeps for ever what is of more value than the re-begged fair copy of that score.[2] Yet should this restoration pain you, I perhaps can forward something you would think a fair return. What?—

Farewell, best Wesendonck! May these lines find you in good health and spirits!

Your

RICHARD WAGNER.

The master was not mistaken in his estimate of his

---

[1] Ludwig Schnorr of Carolsfeld, who died at Dresden on July 21, 1865, at the age of 29, just twenty days after his fourth and last performance of *Tristan* in Munich. See *Prose Works*, IV.

[2] The sketches for the music of *Rheingold*, *Walküre*, and *Siegfried*, so far as the latter had progressed by then; they are mapped out on three "systems," as guide for the subsequent orchestration.

friend's nobility, as we may gather from the letters of both King and artist in the following month.   Ludwig II. wrote from Hohenschwangau :

My dear Herr von Wesendonck !

I hasten to express to you my warmest thanks for the kind relinquishment of Wagner's original score of the Rheingold.—Rest assured that, for my part, I never should have advanced such a claim ; the idea of procuring me the precious score of the glorious work issued from Wagner himself.— I know, you gave friendly asylum to the artist erewhile in his struggles with want and indicible sorrows ; for that I express to you, honoured Sir, my sincerest thanks, since it is in part to your lively sympathy, that we owe the immortal works created by Wagner in Switzerland.—It was a veritable need, to me, to express this to you.

Repeating my thanks, I am with all esteem
                    Your much indebted
                                        LUDWIG.

HOHENSCHWANGAU, *the* 28*th August* 1865.

The envelope, imprinted with the crown and the name *Ludwig*, bears the address : " Sr. Hochwohlgeboren Herrn Otto von Wesendonck."

This letter was forwarded by Wagner to his friend, together with the following lines from Munich, on August 29 :

My dear Wesendonck,

You have much affected and delighted me by your beautiful letter.   My thanks are borne to

you to-day by a mightier than me ; he knows all you
have been, and ever will remain, to me.   It was a
noble solace, to be able to make that understood of
him.

My very heartiest greetings to you ! I still am
very sore.—Total seclusion from the world, and the
most strenuous productivity, to which I shall
exclusively devote myself henceforward, alone can
heal the deep wounds from which I suffer.

Farewell and greet the dear wife most cordially
from

Your faithfully devoted
RICHARD WAGNER.

It should be noted that the King's thanks apply equally
to the *Rheingold* score and to that of *Die Walküre*, since
both were sent him at like time (*Siegfried* was still un-
finished).   Both of these scores had been written with a
pen presented to Wagner by Frau Wesendonck, as we
shall soon be reminded ; this pen is referred to in his letter
to Liszt of June 1854 : " Don't look out for a copyist.
Frau Wesendonck has given me a gold pen of indestructible
virtue, which has turned me once more into a caligraphic
pedant.   The scores will be my most perfect masterpieces
of caligraphy."—

In December 1865 Wagner left Munich in consequence
of the intrigues to which he was a constant victim, and
travelled to the south of France by his doctors' advice.   At
Marseilles he received the news of the sudden death of his
wife Minna on the 25th January 1866 at Dresden, where
she succumbed to a seizure of the heart.   She was buried in

the local churchyard of St. Anne, where the master had a beautiful marble cross erected on her grave.

Just before the production of *Die Meistersinger* at Munich in the year 1868 (June 21) Wagner sent the following lines from thence on June the 1st, presumably accompanied by the pianoforte-score [or perhaps a portrait, or volume, of the real Hans Sachs ?] :

Here, valued Friend, you have a sign of life from me, and, as I hope, a good and friendly one.   May it be received as such, at least, on the "green hill." The faithful old *Sachs* must make his bow, to freshen pleasant memories in you ; no better envoy could I choose, to bring you tidings of myself, my earnest, vivid and sincerely grateful memory of my friends. So let him give his message well.

And now for the news, that I am toiling hard to bring about a really excellent performance of the work ; the joy of full success already braces all my powers.   I can promise my friends the first performance for June the 21st at latest.

In pursuance of a vow I took in times of trouble, I shall not be present at the performances themselves, yet shall diligently guide their spirit down to the final dress-rehearsal.   You would therefore meet at anyrate that spirit, should you journey hither for the birthday of a work once bid to you in such dire need, and tended by you with such faithful patience.   For the rest, my path is that of utmost solitude and retirement, as rest and quiet form my weightiest need in life.

Now warmly greet your honoured wife and children
for me, and remain good to me, as I am always
mindful of and heartily thankful to you as
Your
faithfully devoted
RICHARD WAGNER.

On the 13th July of the same year a letter came from
Tribschen near Lucerne (on the shore of the Lake), where
Wagner resided from 1866 to 1872 :

Dear Wesendonck,
    It much rejoiced me to hear that you really
had followed my invitation and given yourself in
all earnest to the impression of two performances of
the "Meistersinger." I may hope, if only on
account of the excellence of these performances, that
you really had some joy of the thing ; it is impossible
that you can ever have witnessed so good and correct
a performance of so difficult a work ; for—apart
from "Tristan und Isolde" three years ago—this has
been the only one that really gave me joy, myself,
and hope of the formation of a truly German style in
matters operatic. Unfortunately my co-operation—
and in particular the anger inevitable with disturbing
elements—has much overwrought me once more.
After the first performance, which, owing to my
great anxiety about the singers, I had meant to
watch over in secret, I departed for my country
retreat, where I have been ill ever since. Yet I
expect to recover again, and then set to work at

finishing the Nibelungen pieces, which have hitherto remained exactly where I left them over ten years back.—

Your interest has much delighted me, and I beg you in return to be assured of my constant most faithful and grateful recollections of your ancient friendship.
With hearty greetings,
Yours sincerely
RICHARD WAGNER.

Wagner's intention to keep away from the performances of *Die Meistersinger* had been frustrated by the King, who wished the author to sit beside him in the Royal box. At the close of the performance the King commanded him to acknowledge thence the acclamations of the audience. The next day, of course, the Munich newspapers were bursting with indignation at what they called this shameless impudence of the artist's.

From Tribschen came another letter, dated August 21, 1869, accompanied by a French edition of the master's earlier operas :

Dear honoured Friend,
'Tis time that you should have another sign of life from one upon whose life you have inscribed yourself to his lasting grateful recollection.

The fairly compact issue of my earlier operas in French translation, which I herewith send you as a friendly souvenir, offers me a most appropriate opportunity.   If I add to them the "*cinque canti,*" [1]

[1] The *Fünf Gedichte* written by Frau Mathilde Wesendonck and composed by Wagner at Zurich in 1857-58.

it is chiefly for sake of spreading a little smile on the green hill.

After so long and bewildering an interruption, at last I have been so happy as to resume the completion of my Nibelungen pieces, and positively have just ended the third act of " Siegfried." That I have found myself still possessed of the faculty, has filled me with great confidence in my further productivity, and consequently imbued me with the wish for a calm old age. I hope that the resolutions which I have taken will tend to fulfil that wish; in any case it means entire abstention from the excitements and annoyances which the performance of my works has hitherto provided me. Should you wish to hear and see our " Rheingold "—which now seems pretty definitely settled for the end of this month at Munich—you would not find myself there. Despite the fact that these performances will take place in quite another fashion than what I anticipated until a little while ago, I could not prevent the King of Bavaria, to whom I am so uncommonly indebted for the artist-quiet of my life, from having the things set before him. For that matter, everything is being done according to my instructions; the singers, conductors, painters and machinists, have all had to come to me, and take their orders from me ; but to throw myself upon the spot into all the often odious agitation, now too well known to me, I most emphatically declined. Therefore, should you wish to attend the " Rheingold," I believe you will really witness something quite respectable ; nothing has

been spared, to comply with all my technical require-
ments ; [1] that my singers are not precisely gods, you
will probably perceive, even without my drawing your
attention to their humannesses.

Begging you to remember me most cordially to
your dear honoured wife, I remain with ever grateful
and truly friendly memory

Yours sincerely

RICHARD WAGNER.

A letter from Tribschen of January 5, 1870, contains the
following passages of general interest :

— — I have now assembled round me quite a host
of relics of my past, which had hitherto been scattered
heedless far and wide.   Thus I now possess the
capital oil-portraits of my mother, my uncle [Adolt
Wagner] and my stepfather [Ludwig Geyer] : of the
second I have laboriously collected all his printed
writings, of the last some letters and a very charming
comedy [the *Slaughter of the Innocents*].   Of my own
life, many a souvenir from earliest days has been
recovered.   In times of untold stir it has afforded
me a soothing refuge, since about four years, to
dictate my entire Life, which I will bequeath some
day to him who shall frame my biography — long
after my death,—unless the magnitude and repulsive-
ness of the current distortions should decide me even
earlier to give some qualified person the necessary
material from my dictations to correct single points.

[1] The first performance of *Das Rheingold* did not take place until Sep. 22,
after all, and under conditions to which Wagner alludes in no flattering terms
in Vol. V. of the *Prose Works*, p. 311.

To save this manuscript from disappearance, it lately occurred to me to have half a dozen copies of it printed at my own expense. One of the first proof-sheets, just received, I now forward you herewith, but with the earnest request not to view it as a presumptuous appeal to your sympathy.

Whatever else may occur to interest you in my life and doings, shall always be faithfully transmitted to you. I needs must wish to reach a good old age, as my duties in life have infinitely increased, and only now are my painful experiences to be requited by that repose to which I shall owe at last, I hope, the completion of all the works in which I was so sadly hindered in my bygone life—almost with solitary exception of the time when I lived in your neighbourhood and under shelter of your friendship.

The "Götterdämmerung" is begun : after a little rest and self-collection, "Parzival" shall follow ; whilst much besides is shaping hopefully within me for further creation.—

So, Friends on the Green Hill, be heartily greeted for this new year also from

Your devoted
RICHARD WAGNER.

Do you recognise the pen with which I have written this letter?—It still is going, and got smoothly over the "Meistersinger" too !

A last letter from Tribschen, of December 4, 1870, was accompanied by some of Wagner's essays :

Here, honoured Friend, something quite new from the wilds !—" About Conducting " I haven't sent you, as the " Judaism " aroused your ire, and I was afraid those articles, as well, would not quite suit you. But you have a right to hear nothing but agreeables from me ; consequently it is my duty to be careful.

The pianoforte-score of "Siegfried " will probably appear toward Easter. The "Götterdämmerung " I expect to have finished next year. To see my great work carried out in exact accordance with my will, remains my only aim in traffic with the world. I feel certain of your aid in this.

I hope it goes well with yourself and all life on the " green hill." It always delights me to hear good news from you.

With the request to remember me most kindly to your honoured wife, I greet you with old and grateful devotion !

Your
RICHARD WAGNER.

The Wesendonck household removed in 1870 to Dresden, and later to Berlin. The bond of friendship with Wagner remained unbroken. As Frau Mathilde Wesendonck has told us in the *Allgemeine Musik-Zeitung* of January 1896, " After his second marriage, Wagner's first visit with his wife was paid to ' Mariafeld ' near Zurich, the residence of the Wille's, and to the ' green hill ' at Enge. To the latter he brought the children too. Not one of the

Festivals at Bayreuth did we ever miss.   Down to his death we remained in friendly correspondence with the master."

In November 1896 Otto Wesendonck died in Berlin, at the age of 82 ; he was buried in his family vault at Bonn on the Rhine.   In the *Bayreuther Blätter* of December '96 an editorial article pays the fullest tribute to the memory of a man whose noble qualities are unforgettable by all who knew him.   But more durable than marble or eulogium, his character will go down to posterity as the prototype of one of the chief personages in *Die Meistersinger*, for Richard Wagner wrote to him in July 1862 :

> " *In the affection with which I have treated the part of* Pogner—*in the music too— it really is to me as if I had been setting up a monument to a friend.*"

LETTERS OF RICHARD WAGNER

TO

MALWIDA VON MEYSENBUG

RICHARD WAGNER'S correspondence with Malwida von Meysenbug[1] in reality commenced at about the same time as his acquaintance with the Wesendoncks, for his first note to her was written in 1852, in answer to an enthusiastic letter which she had sent to him as a total stranger. As she tells us in her article in the August number of *Cosmopolis*, 1896,—in which the following letters first appeared,—Frl. v. Meysenbug made Wagner's personal acquaintance in London at the house of friends one evening in 1855, and renewed it at a Paris concert in 1859. Her reminiscences of their further meetings in Paris have been reproduced in an earlier chapter of the present book, so that we may proceed at once to the master's letters themselves, which partly fill the gaps in the correspondence with Herr Wesendonck.

I.

PARIS, 20*th May* 1860.

Dear Lady,

Your letter received to-day was doubly welcome, as it brought me not only the enclosure, but a renewal of your address. I wanted to write you yesterday, but could not find it. . . .

[1] See page 84.

Now, at last, for what I had to tell you first. I beg you to present my best respects to Madame S.,[1] and tell her how particularly grieved I am at not being able as yet to send her back the money so kindly advanced me, as not the smallest change has taken place in my situation. From no side have I had a tittle of relieving news. I therefore leave it to Madame S., as she unfortunately is so largely interested in my situation, to address her own inquiries to Paris. Only, I should prefer that under any circumstances the appearance should be maintained as if I had not been made acquainted with the proposal to recoup me for the loss entailed by my concerts. I could easily beg Madame S., whom I considered very rich and fully in the position to afford me the needful relief out of her own pocket—in view of her especial predisposition I very well might ask her for a loan, which I have every prospect of being able to repay in a few years' time. A collection with the object of making me a *present* of the forfeit sum, however, I could in nowise have invited, as I know how little genuine faith is reposed in a man who turns to others for *pecuniary* help, and how his situation, be it what it may, is measured from that instant by *one* standard. The extraordinary will ever remain extraordinary, and uncomprehended. Accordingly I implore Madame S. to preserve the look that without my knowing it she

[1] A rich friend of Frl. v. Meysenbug's, who had lent Wagner money to help defray the enormous deficit on his Paris and Brussels concerts of Jan., Feb. and March 1860. Two other of Frl. v. M.'s lady friends in Paris then proposed to get up a private subscription for him ; with what results, we shall presently see.

was acquainted by you during her stay in Paris with the losses I had confidentially imparted to you. By this means the delicacy of my sympathetic lady friend will fortunately not be wounded. . . .

[Here follow the reasons of Wagner's removal to Paris, chiefly concerned with his wife.]

— — I now perceive that I should have done wiser to leave my household affairs in a provisory state for awhile ; all the more so, as my personal wish was not the determinant factor. My present concern is to see how I can mend the error. From time to time unusual windfalls, almost natural in my position toward the world, have come to rectify the faultiness of my arrangements. Such I have ever accepted on the principle that those who busy themselves for me, gain more thereby than I myself ; as I seek rest and happiness no longer, but only breathing-space for new labours, from which *I* reap the least enjoyment. Just now it seems that things will not fit in so easily ; everything, even the promised and wellnigh secured, leaves me waiting in vain. Were I to yield to my inner prompting, I should free myself entirely with a single step, for Possession has never had a trace of power over me. Should you ever hear that Fate has raised me above every other consideration in the disposition of my outward life, than that of my own fancy, you would at like time hear that I had voluntarily chosen total poverty and retreat. Be assured of that, best Friend. . . .

[Personal inquiries relating to the recipient.]

— — That you hope to come back to Paris next autumn, you will believe how glad I am to hear it! If you still remain in *chains*, however, take comfort again and again from the question of the Princess Leonore: And who is happy? For my part I assure you that I merely look on at the world, to learn how it comports itself towards a man of my stamp, and how it understands to profit of him: whether it will accord him the space, determinable only by the laws of his own nature, for development of his activity; or how much it will haggle away therefrom. I often can smile at it all; tho' I cannot deny that, as a sentient being, I am involved enough in the game to feel pains of all kinds under the experiment. Thus much is certain: I have already created much more than were requisite, had I wanted to feel a little ease myself at times. But that's the way!

Farewell and accept my hearty thanks for your friendship, also for the Turkish tobacco, which affords me at anyrate the prospect of periodic oriental ease.

Your R. WAGNER.

A brief note came ten days later, asking for news, as this was his only hope of pulling through. But the Parisian friends hung fire, and on June the 22nd, 1860, Frl. v. Meysenbug received another letter:

2.

Best Friend,

My warmest thanks for your friendly letter. You were perfectly right in attributing my lengthy silence to my gloomy mood. In my life I have had to do battle with much unpleasantness, and the ironical gift of total impecuniousness, added to so obstinate a temperament as mine, has prepared me nasty conflicts at all times. No one grasps this wholly, and yet it may be seized with both hands ; for instance, were any one to take a good look at me now, when I ought to be snatching at everything that promises to lighten my burden, and yet can stoop so little to concessions that I yesterday declared to the Director of the Opéra here that the Tannhäuser shall be given either as it is (without a ballet in the 2nd act) or not at all. What this obstinacy means, now that you know my situation, you best may judge. For I must confess that in all the 8 years during which my operas have been given in Germany, a condition like my present one has never yet been known to me ; I always had something coming in, and could manage in the way I lived. But now my older operas are quite played out, my new ones hindered, enormous losses and— no one to help me !—All I ask for, is credit during a stoppage ! Impossible ! I unbosom myself, and gain nothing by it but exposure. In the journals I

read that I have been given 10,000 francs, and the
mockery with which they dress the news is all that I
get of it.   My Russian General arrives ; it trans-
pires that there can be no question of Petersburg for
next winter, as I should have to be there at the
same time as I am needed here ; consequently—done
for !   I have had to stave off claims on me from one
day to another, the most annoying upsets in the
house, agitation and insomnia of my wife.   She is
ordered to Soden, for the baths, and I can find no
money for it.   So it goes on, and will last for half a
year at least, if *last* it can.   And to me this happens,
who am always being told of the enthusiasm I am
arousing here and there and everywhere, etc.   Of
all the people to whom I have addressed myself,
Madame S. must rank with fullest right in my eyes
as the only creature that could really brace herself to
help.   As things have turned, I truthfully assure
you I have learnt to value Mme. S. most highly.
When I remember how you came to me on that day
of peril, and handed me the heavy sum required, I
cannot but admit that she was the only one to prove
her staunchness.   Please tell her that.   Don't be
astonished at my uttering no words of praise to you,
although I had to recognise in Mme. S. your work
alone ; for that goes without saying, whereas Mme. S.
did not.   Of the subscription there can be no more
talk ; here everything has rotted root and crop.   What
should have been the work of two days at the
outside, has dragged itself through two indiscreet
months into the journals, and unfortunately also into

the hands of Fould ; which, alone, is sufficient reason
for declining any benefit.

．　　　．　　　．　　　．　　　．　　　．

Let us drop that. To me there remains nothing
but my debt, my thanks, and my sorrow for
Madame S. (not to be able to repay her at once), and
further—the hell from which I haven't the remotest
idea as yet of how to get redeemed. It is still a
matter of 5000 francs, the balance of my deficit,
before I arrive at the performance of Tannhäuser.

Nevertheless I have been able to devote my
sympathy to Garibaldi also, and assure you that I
always take the evening-paper with great eagerness ;
as you very rightly observe, it was the only thing
that could refresh even me, as the artistic element is
the most incapable of all in positions like mine ; for
one must *be* free, for that, not merely want to. Nor
can I, in such moods, gain freedom even for artistic
reading, and Plutarch has again been my solitary
distraction. I had been much struck, indeed, upon
reading his life of Timoleon once more, on which I
lit by hazard. This life has the quite remarkable
distinction, that it really ends completely happily, an
altogether exceptional case in history. It really does
one good to see that such a thing was possible for
once; yet, remembering the fate of every other noble
thing, it cannot prevent me from recognising such a
case as but a decoy-bird set by the World-demon.
This possibility had to remain open, if such countless
numbers were to be misled about the actual import of
the world. Had this possibility been nowhere pre-

sented, one might almost assume that there would have been a shorter road for us to take to where we Occidentals—so it seems—shall only arrive by a very long circuit. Well: how many points of contact there were, to make me lately bracket Garibaldi with Timoleon. He still is lucky! Should it be possible for him to be spared the utmost bitter dregs? From my heart I wish it. Yet I often tremble when I behold him as a mere fly in the huge European spider's-web. But many possibilities stand open: perhaps the fly is too big and strong. Upon his *Folk* he should not count, but very much upon his Alpine chasseurs! For the rest, let treason help him, and the prudence to direct it. Through the baseness of the bad one sometimes triumphs o'er their insolence.

That you are coming to Paris, is a great consolation to me. I cannot possibly get away from here, and shall thank my stars if I even get my poor wife to the baths. Farewell, and accept the best wishes of

Your R. WAGNER.

Through the generous intervention of Mme. Kalergis (subsequently Mme. von Muchanoff) very soon after the above letter, Wagner's pecuniary affairs were brought into something like order for awhile; but, although we have seen him declining Wesendonck's kind offer of assistance in February 1861, the *Tannhäuser* fiasco in March reduced him to fresh misery, and unfortunately it would seem from the letter of June 25, 1861, that Wesendonck himself was temporarily in difficulties. However that may be, on July

25, 1861, Wagner again writes to Frl. v. Meysenbug, this time from the Prussian Embassy in Paris :

3.

— — — The worst is over. I will not dwell on the history of my last month ; that sort of thing is only fit to be forgotten ! It was no use at last; I had to urge my diplomatic friends here to some seriousness. With toil and trouble—but much good will (as I can but testify)—the first necessities were furnished, and I am happy to say that my wife marked little of my real distress. After we had lived through four more ghastly days in the rooms, she set off comfortably a fortnight since, with the parrot. The Prussian ambassador invited me to be his guest for as long as I still must stay in Paris, which I willingly accepted —particularly on account of the beautiful garden with high trees and black swans. I am treated as one of the family, have my grand piano in a lovely, lofty salon, and could make myself fairly at home if only the friendly signs I yet may meet were not almost too late in coming ! Beyond a fleeting ease— especially engendered by the pleasing absence of noise—no sense of wellbeing of any kind will abide with me. My eyes are always full of tears, and the whole affair seems more empty and oppressive to me every day ! Alone, to be quite alone, is finally my only refuge.

Der fliegende Holländer is progressing but slowly

in French ; ready or not ready, I am determined to depart on Monday evening. I shall bid my wife adieu again at Soden for a day. Gladly would I get out of Liszt's invitation, but I hear that it would make him utterly miserable if I didn't come. Then on to Vienna, where I probably shall stay a little longer. If I cast a look at my Tristan score, as yet I can't deem the thing possible !

So you must comfort yourself, dear good lady, with my having escaped the extreme once again. That I have left much behind me, I alas ! feel more and more ; two precious years have been clean squandered, and I feel extraordinarily weary. But what I have lost for art, perhaps I have won for life, a last and deeply-graven lesson : not to try and force what will not fit.

Farewell, and remain ever friendly to

Your R. WAGNER.

Till August 6, Weimar.   Then Vienna, k.k. Hofoperntheater.

On the 13th September, 1861, Wagner at last replies from Vienna.

4.

Best Friend,

I received all your letters, and thank you for them most cordially. Don't insist on a regular correspondence with me, and be assured that you will thereby spare yourself much sorrow. But write often !   It then will be possible for you from time to time to nurse agreeable imaginings about my lot, which you would have to recognise as wrong at once if I wrote you often. Brief and true! It is always the old, old story—also the old illusion, that something might turn out well at last!

The Weimar festival was of absolutely no importance : only Liszt was very charming, and his hospitality, which I shared with half musical Germany, delightful. But rather too many people. It would often happen that I had to relate the whole history of my life to some fresh person each half-hour. For the most part ridiculous! Everywhere little talent, much foolishness. Music often very bad. Liszt's Faust, however, altogether excellent. Thus, always what the few alone can do. The crowd a mere disturbance.

Well, here I sit waiting for the return of a tenor-voice into the throat of my projected Tristan-singer. Ander—my tenor—after a three-months' hoarseness, hasn't recovered control of his voice yet, is afraid of losing it completely, particularly if he has to practise such a trying rôle as Tristan this winter. To admit the truth a little to myself, I can but think the execution of my project impossible for this winter. Thus do things stand! You may therefore judge the bliss in which I hover here, where I simply do not know which way to turn. Whether and how help can be obtained, is more than doubtful, and in the few hours that belong to me I take counsel with myself as to what is to be decided on. For the moment I can hit on no way out at all.

From Paris I hear absolutely nothing.   What am I there ?   Silence everywhere else, and—nothing left me but the heartiest surfeit and loathing of all I do and ply ! . . . .

It is not appointed me, to scrape through lightly. So I again am living both dearly and miserably at once. God knows what a fix I am in !   Indeed the most sensible thing would be, for a gentle end soon to be put to me !   The world is thoroughly contrary to me.

Was I right not to write to you ?   What will you hear, saving trouble ?   The malady has become so chronic with me, that it probably can never be cured. I lack all footing : not even with one toe do I stand firm.   Let us leave the misery ! . . .

Child—see very black indeed, when you look at me, and you'll always see me in the true light !

Then—perhaps I shall be able to console you, for once in a way, with a brighter letter.   Adieu !   A thousand deep-felt thanks for your friendship !

Your R. W.

After a long interval without any tidings, Frl. v. Meysenbug received the following :

5.

BIEBRICH ON THE RHINE, 12th March 1862.

My dear Lady,

Please don't be cross with me !   You see, at last I come unbidden, to shew you, by my writing of my own accord once more, that I also had never forgotten you.   Have thanks for your fidelity.

To Malwida von Meysenbug

In effect, dear friend, I was so beset that I really had some scruples about giving my friends useless pain by news from me. During the whole of this latter time I had but a single period when I actually existed. This was when I shut myself up in Paris, in the most execrable circumstances, as if for my last chance of life, and wrote my Meistersinger poem in four weeks. At the end of January I had finished it, and my next concern was to find a refuge in which to compose its music. That I have at last arranged, with untold difficulties, here at Biebrich ; which took up all my time until to-day, in constant war with disagreeables and the worst of humour. To-morrow, however, I hope to begin the composition. My object is to have the whole thing ready by late-autumn, so that it may go the round of all the German theatres next winter, with which I don't intend to fash myself at all. This resolution was my only safety. For such an undertaking I could claim the requisite advances from my publisher to keep me for a year of work. The month of work in Paris was my happiest, but I could keep up the spell only when I let my eyes roam neither left nor right ; at last I saw no more human beings, nothing but Garçons and Concierges. The poem has given me prodigious joy ; I believe it is my choicest product. I will have it printed toward the end of summer ; till when, alas ! I cannot give it you to read. Yet, here is a sample. Sachs cobbles by night at his stall, and sings the while.

[Hans Sachs' song from Act II.]

Well ! What more do you want ? You have verses now ! For what concerns my other life, I keep men off as far as possible ; you will guess that from the choice of my retreat. Above all, I take good care to have no intercourse henceforth with theatre and opera-house ; I can get light to create for this people, only when I don't see it. . . .

What you write me about Bakunin [1] has interested me much ; I could see the whole man before me. He is, and remains, a colossal chap. One must really take the bear as book, to account for such a nature. Röckel, too, has been let out of prison at last : he has behaved splendidly, and shewn an unshakable firmness ; he boasts a bear's nature too, and is delighted at the chance of agitating and politicising again to his heart's content. In truth I have nothing against it, and am glad to see such people at their handicraft. But really it becomes too much a metier, and for that they hit on a routine of thought and view which I often have to envy them, though I can find no actual substance in it. However, that doesn't seem at all required. The formalism of Politics has such a many-headed name, that it will always look like something. There's no help for it : I no longer see the masses, but only individuals ; and there each person ever thinks his way, and I think mine !—Adieu, dear friend ! From his whole heart greets you   Your R. W.

---

[1] Michael Bakunin, who was seriously involved in the Dresden insurrection of 1849, had now been liberated from his Siberian prison, and had arrived in London. See Wagner's *Letters to August Roeckel* and *Letters to Uhlig*.

6.

BIEBRICH, *June* 15, '62.

Best thanks, dear Friend, for your most interesting letter ! Certainly no one has more beautifully conceived and outlined the high and only pregnant possibility of a political development of European mankind. Your idea of Rome has much impressed me,[1] and I sought at once for what I myself could do to help it forward.

Dear friend, thus much is certain : the Messias-myth is that of the profoundest bearing on all earthly effort. The Jews were waiting for the liberator, the Messias, who should establish the kingdom of David, bring justice with him, before all else, but also grandeur, power, security against oppression. Well, everything concurred : born in Bethlehem, of the seed of David, the prophecy of the three Kings, etc., festal welcome to Jerusalem, palms strewn—there He stands, all listen and He proclaims to them : " My kingdom is not of this world ! Renounce your wishes ; there lies the only freedom and redemption ! " Believe me, all our political liberation-mongers appear to me, in private, like those Jews. But ! we can tell that to the veriest few, of course, and accordingly—look on ! The special stimulus of Italy, however, I don't deny.

---

[1] At that time, when Italy was struggling for reunion, Frl. v. M. had suggested to Wagner that Rome should be a neutral capital of intellect and spirit.

Your projects of a Florentine settlement are most respectable. What may not happen to me yet! I can decide on nothing even a month in advance. Most certainly I wish and seek for nothing more upon this earth than leisure for work, as that alone can make my presence on it either explicable or acceptable to me. Performances I can entirely forego. I'm silently plodding at a plan to die to all men, and somewhere quietly, as a departed spirit, work out my artistic drafts and nothing else. Otherwise I shall never come to rest. . . .

Naturally I propose to stay here as long as I can anyhow manage, for my work. It is progressing, and satisfactorily—but I can't work fast : firstly, because of unavoidable outer and inner interruptions ; secondly, because no single bar can give me pleasure, that does not owe its origin to a really good idea. Those, however, one cannot command.

7.

VIENNA, 12th December 1862.

Dearest Lady, before the middle of December— till when a letter might reach you yet in London— I certainly expected to have got so much the better of my temper, as to be able to write you properly. Now I am left with nothing but the anxiety lest it should be too late for news of mine to catch you ; consequently I determine to let you have these lines at least, even though they constitute no letter. Yet, as much as possible in the briefest space !

To Malwida von Meysenbug

I could not retain my Rhine work-room. The publisher left me in the lurch. A quarter of a year of total dislocation, useless efforts, untold want, set in. Final necessity of resuming outward undertakings, this time with the energy of sheer despair. On the 26th Dec. and 1st January two first grand concerts in Vienna, with fragments from Nibelungen and Meistersinger. Mid-January first performance of Tristan, ensuring star-week for *Schnorrs* (admirable). Then concerts again. Then perhaps the same concerts in Berlin. If not, perhaps to Petersburg for concerts ; whither invited. (Simply to procure myself funds for a few years of rest !)

Gladly would I come to Italy, and perhaps shall come indeed. It's drumming in my head : after such pedlary, nothing but Italy can really reward and set me up again. Let me have news ; I'm here till end of January.

At present wholly upset ; unspeakable weariness of life, daily astonishment that I am still alive ; dæmonic riddle there ! Once more, maybe for sake of a few fair years in Italy !

Adieu, dearest friend ; have no doubt of my sincerest sympathy ! From my heart

Your R. WAGNER.

After an unusually long interval, during which Frl. v. Meysenbug had passed a winter at Florence and gone on to Rome, a letter came from Penzing, near Vienna, dated June 22, 1863 :

8.

Dearest, best Lady !

You indeed are a friend that does not take affront at once, if a letter stays unanswered, but writes charmingly on ! And honourably shall you be mentioned for it ! Your last letter but one I received on my return from Russia, here in Vienna. I hardly knew what to say to your assuming that I should have declined the invitation of the Petersburg Philharmonic Society (a posse of German musicians), out of Polish patriotism, and preferred to starve in Germany ! [1]

So I had to leave you looking in amazement at my going there, and devising measures for my giving better guarantees of my political conscientiousness in future.—Ah, best friend ! I'm an utterly frivolous being : I'm a fanatic of quiet, nothing else. At Petersburg and Moscow, in the midst of my triumphs, the midst of true joy at the really incredibly fine performances I brought about with the musicians there—in the midst of acclamations not surpassed for warmth and enthusiasm by Vienna itself—at bottom I had but one fancy in mind, the hut and garden with a few fine old trees, which I had left to others everywhere in Germany on my departure, and I meant to conquer for myself by

---

[1] Frl. v. M. explains that this was not her meaning, but she had merely suggested that the trouble and commotion in Poland might have altered Wagner's plans.

everything that went on round me. Arrived back in Vienna, direct from Petersburg, I called on no one, but merely spied out for the longed-for house and garden : from the Rhine delays—found of a sudden at Penzing (at Penzing !)—the house and garden, quiet, pleasant ! I rent, and furnish agreeably to my taste, with my own money—or rather, what I have been left of it—, am alone, have found good and sympathetic servants, and now am hunting out my work again !

Admit it ! With such a man there's nothing to be done ! Just give me up ! While I still was seeking, I thought to myself : God, if Liszt were suddenly to write that he had found you a beautiful house and garden in Rome—would you go there after all ? Well : not freely ! Why ? I cannot stand excitement any longer, especially just now. I have been so shamefully robbed of precious years of work and productivity, that I believe such a charge of altogether new impressions, as Rome and Italy, would throw me wholly out of gear. Proudhon somewhere says, in opposition to those who looked to railways for such marvels in the intellectual training of mankind : " le génie est sédentaire." And so it is, believe me ! Whom a little suffices not to build his world, still less will he be capable to do it out of much. Yet I say all this with a certain bitterness of disclaimer. Heavens ! how gladly would I also stretch myself out there, for once, and let a wondrous outer world react upon me ! But everyone has his dæmon, and mine is a horridly despotic beast ; he yokes me to his purpose out and out.

Tell me, child! how can I get a copy of my Meistersinger poem to you ? Please inquire, and let me know. I'm living here entirely without company, and wish for nothing but to be left alone, to be able to complete my job without interruption. Whether I perform anything of it, or not, has become at last a matter of total indifference to me. Yes, it thoroughly suited me, after my enormous exertion, that I hadn't to take up Tristan here again at once (Frau Dustmann is ill). After all, one must get along with what one is to one's own self : to be able to have a little respect for oneself, is therefore the one thing needful.

But of course, one mustn't be given such glowing accounts of wonders like the Michael Angelo, etc. ; [1] for then one's heart grows heavy—to be sure! Moreover, for your tranquillising I will tell you that I read an Austrian paper every day, instinctively side with the Polish insurrection, and in general am falling into many of my old weaknesses. But I feel like Goethe : for a proper political fervour I haven't *hate* enough, and without that one contents no party. God ! do you believe, then, that there is a single educated person in Petersburg to whom the Polish events are not a horror, or who does not feel and speak about them just as you and I ? But " Politics " —" Government," and whatever else the Devil's stuff may call itself—eh ! that's another thing. And

[1] Frl. v. M. had written from Rome about the Sixtine Chapel.

believe me, I and you, we are not made for it ; even
Garibaldi is not, and still less Bakunin, but quite
certainly Louis Napoleon. And who would measure
himself with him ? The Devil !

Little Tausig is my only companion, a sensible
young man, quite out of the common.

If you've been able to make any sense of these
lines (it's shocking weather out-of-doors) I shall be
heartily delighted. *Where* should I have to begin,
to write you rationally !

A thousand cordial greetings !

Your R. WAGNER.

After numerous letters had remained unanswered, Frl. v.
Meysenbug gave up writing to Wagner, not knowing
where to find him, till finally a letter came from Tribschen,
dated July 1, 1867 :

9.

Dearest Lady !

Wahn ! Wahn ! überall Wahn !

That's now my theme !—That you should imagine
I didn't answer you because things were going *well*
with me, is one of the most singular quid-pro-quo's
that could arise. Your letters, even those to Penzing
(near Vienna), while you were revelling in Italy,
found me in a permanent state of dissolution and
despair as to how to smooth this beast of a life
enough to get at least for once a year of rest for
working in. To have written you then, when I was
daily on the leap from one obstruction to another,

would have been sheer folly, believe me! Then I
went to Munich: now that was fine, was it not?
My child!! Have you the least idea of what I had
to go through there at last? Or do you really think
that my having good board and lodging, albeit I was
torn and dragged through every puddle because of
that unheard-of favour, made it *well* with me? God,
I was ready at any moment to cast it all away again;
the only thing to hold me back, was sincere affection
for my young, mysterious and perhaps miraculous
friend, for whom I have suffered more than for any
human soul before. But—how could I tell you that
so lightly? I have saved him, and in him still hope
to have preserved for the world one of my best
works! You heard of my leaving Munich, in
December 1865. I went to Geneva, breathed again,
cast a longing glance at the south of France or Italy,
to find a haven where to work again at last. Well!
so I thought of you, and also looked around for you;
for, my resolution formed to work again, "well"-
going glimmered up; and when it goes well with
me, then I think of my friends—not the other way,
when it goes badly. You foolish person!—How to
discover your whereabouts? At last you had kept a
long silence. Then one day I find a card left by
Herzen, who had called on me with a young lady
[his daughter]; on the back of the card the lady had
written good wishes from you. I was told they
would call again. Then I sought out Herzen himself, who was stopping a long way off from me: the
message from you was a finger of Fate. I did not

find him in, twice and three times over.   He didn't
let that move him to pay another call on me.   That
vexed me.[1]

Furthermore, the Devil was playing his pranks
again behind my back : I durst not go too far from
Munich, if I would prevent the young King's abdi-
cation.   At the beginning of April 1866, I took a
lease of this country house near Lucerne, where I
have settled down for 6 years' work.[2]   Horrible times
had to be endured even last summer, but I got
through with the music of the Meistersinger.[3]   Another work finished at last !   To Munich I only pay
visits.   The Meistersinger is to come out at the
beginning of next winter.   To *that* performance you
must come, do you hear ?   It is my masterwork ;
not one comes up to it.

Now you know all, however little I have written
you.   Your letters, especially from Rome, I have
often read again.   In everything you women are
much better off ; delight in everything, an environment, an impression, always comes easier to you.
Only reflect that I have felt, and still feel in fact, a
positive horror of having, or being *forced*, to take
delight in such things.   Whenever I tried it of yore,
I straightway fell ill and wretched—especially was
this the case with me in Italy.   I never am well,
saving when I have full rest for work.   Everything

---

[1] Herzen, father of the little Olga mentioned in a previous chapter, had
been summoned to Vevey, at the other end of the Lake of Geneva, as Frl. v.
Meysenbug informs us.

[2] And where he remained, in fact, till April 1872.

[3] The full *orchestral* score was not finished until October 20, 1867.

outside but hinders, hinders, only hinders me. But —just that " rest " was very hard, again, to compass. You sent me somebody to Munich? Eh, how precious quickly I had flown thence! Here I am, ever somewhat ailing, with a big and a little dog, a good young musician as secretary,[1] in the wonderful world of mountains, and compose " Wahn! Wahn! Ueberall Wahn!" Now let me hear something of you, as I really find myself a little "well." From my heart   Your RICHARD WAGNER.

[1] Hans Richter.

LETTERS OF RICHARD WAGNER

TO

FRAU ELIZA WILLE

BETWEEN four and five English miles from Zurich, Herr François Wille and his wife Eliza had been living since the early winter of 1851 at Mariafeld. A year or two before her marriage, Frau Wille had made Richard Wagner's acquaintance at an evening-party in Dresden, 1843, but had since lost sight of him until Professor Ettmüller, who saw a good deal of the composer at Zurich, in the spring of 1852 informed the Willes that Wagner was dwelling in their neighbourhood.

I.

Honoured Lady!

I have just come into the country near town, to recover from my late exertions under the influence, it is to be hoped, of fair weather and open air. Among my restoratives I in any case shall count a visit, and with your permission several visits, to Mariafeld ; indeed it would not have needed your friendly invitation, to determine me. Only, I should not wish to leave my scarcely-entered refuge quite so soon as next Sunday, and therefore beg you on behalf of myself and my wife, who is very grateful for your greetings, not to expect us till a later Sunday.

Begging you to convey my best compliments to Herr Wille, I am

Yours gratefully and faithfully

RICHARD WAGNER.

ZURICH, 18*th May*, 1852.

Shortly afterwards Wagner paid his visit, which was followed by an intimacy with Herr and Frau Wille apparently only second to that with the Wesendoncks, with whom both parties were on terms of friendship. We have already seen that in August 1858 the master left Zurich for good, and we have been able to follow his course pretty closely at the hand of our first two groups of letters. Frau Wille also received letters from him during that period, but as they dealt almost exclusively with private matters, the next she publishes is of the early Spring of 1864 :

2.

Esteemed Lady,

I beg you to consult our friends as to whether they think it possible to take me in this summer. In that manner the goal of my latest troubles might yet be reached. These arose through my endeavour to secure non-interruption of my work by obviating the necessity of a long art-tour in Russia, for this year, through borrowing a capital equivalent to the sum to be earned there. The awful plight into which I fell through not being able to obtain this money, after Russia had been thrown over, is on the point of being smoothed. People who have me and my situation under their eyes, and can judge at close quarters, have found it possible to comprehend, excuse, and therefore also remedy.

As in any case, however, I see myself compelled to abandon my residence here, owing to its proved too great expense, the first question is to secure a quiet and becoming shelter for the time I still require to end my Meistersinger. From a purely practical point of view, this would be found the fittest in the house of the family W[esendonck]. Certainly there have arisen grounds against a permanent removal thither. Nor is that what I suggest. After finishing my work—which, with total freedom from disturbance, can be effected by the end of this summer—I shall turn my steps to Petersburg, probably to remain there for good : should I not decide on this latter course, of a definitive migration to Petersburg, I should probably withdraw to some of my relatives, as I sorely need to lean upon a family.

Just now, on the contrary, it is a mere matter of a speedy refuge for the continuance of my work, which otherwise could hardly escape being given up entirely and for ever.

Well, as earlier invitations to make my abode with them for awhile have not as yet been actually revoked by my friends, I knit therewith the weightiest, nay, the definitely last attempt to save my work.

It is purely for Frau W. to say, whether my workroom shall be arranged in the principal building, or in the little neighbouring house I occupied before.

A little necessary furniture still stands at my disposal, and could be used as a help. For the rest, I ask nothing but food and service. In no other way will I become a burden.

Now I beg you to make inquiries as soon as possible, and address myself to you in the first place to ascertain if my wish has any likelihood of being fulfilled.

My heartiest thanks for your many and great proofs of interest ; and I beg you, under any circumstances, to preserve me your friendship.

Yours most sincerely
RICHARD WAGNER.

PENZING, NEAR VIENNA, 14*th March* 1864.

As the proposal could not be realised just then, Wagner wrote to Herr Wille, inviting himself to stay for a short while at Mariafeld. Herr Wille was at Constantinople, on a trip ; but before Frau Wille had time to reply, Wagner arrived in person. With the assistance of her two sons, and subsequently of a married sister, the lady hospitably entertained him until the return of her husband.

In the *Deutsche Rundschau* for March 1887—in which these letters first appeared—Frau Wille gives a highly interesting account of this visit of about a month, during which she truly played the part of mother to the genius in his very darkest hour. A few brighter days dawned with Herr Wille's return; then letters came for Wagner, apparently with serious news, and at the end of April he departed. From Bâle, where he made his first halt, he sent a line proposing to return ere long, and perhaps to settle down close by them. Frau Wille replied at once to the master's address at Stuttgart, regretting that she could not agree to his plan : by return of post she received the following letter :

3.

My very dear Friend,
        I answer you briefly, because I have already
said so much to you.—Your wish, not to see me at
Mariafeld again, concurs with my own feeling about
it. Let us terminate that stormy night of fever,
which even the loveliest sunshine out-of-doors refused
to brighten, and draw a veil over the changeful pictures
it brought forth. My immediate fate is still uncertain ;
but a doctor, whom I have consulted, recommends
me Cannes : the Eckert family is amiable to me, and
not unimportant consequences may flow from the
acquaintance I have made with Baron Gall, Intendant
of the Court-theatre here. We know that the
Christian virtue Hope has mostly been my undoing
whenever I have yielded to it. An opera-performance
which I attended yesterday, for the first time since
ever so long, put me mortally out of humour.
        My sincerest greetings to your sister ! You must
both forgive me the unspeakable uneasiness I caused
you, dear ladies.
        I shall write to Wille, amicably informing him of
my resolve to give up Mariafeld.
        Please write to me, some day, from Hamburg :
address to Stuttgart, c/o Kapellmeister Eckert.
        Farewell, dear noble friend ! Never will the
warmth of my gratitude cool down : never !—
        From the bottom of my heart   Your
                        RICHARD WAGNER.
STUTTGART, 2nd May 1864.

L

Meanwhile events had been most rapidly developing. Two or three days after Wagner's departure from Mariafeld, Herr von Pfistermeister arrived there ; as private secretary to King Ludwig II. (who had inherited the throne of Bavaria on March the 10th at the age of barely 18½ years), he had been sent in search of Wagner to Vienna, and thence had tracked him to Mariafeld. Now furnished with Wagner's address at Stuttgart, he seems to have reached there on May the 3rd (if not, late on the 2nd itself), and borne the master off at once to Munich, as may be judged by the date of the next letter :

4.

MUNICH, 4th *May* '64, Bairischer Hof.

Dearest Friend,
    I should be the most ungrateful of men, did I not announce to you at once my boundless good fortune !
    You know that the young King of Bavaria had me searched for. To-day I was conducted to him. Alas ! he is so handsome and intelligent, so splendid and so full of soul, that I fear lest his life should vanish like a fleeting dream of gods in this vulgar world. He loves me with the depth and glow of a first love : he knows and fathoms everything about me, and understands me as my soul. He wills that I shall always stay with him, work, rest, perform my works ; he will give me all I need therefor ; I am to finish the Nibelungen, and he will have it performed according to my wish. I am to be my own unfettered master, not Kapellmeister, nothing but myself and

his friend. And all this he means quite seriously
and strictly, as if we two, yourself and I, were talking
to each other. All trouble shall be taken from me ;
I am to have whatever I want—only, near him am I
to abide.

What do you say to it?—What do you say?—Is
it not unheard of?—Can it be aught save a dream ?
Imagine how moved I am !

A thousand hearty wishes! My happiness is so
great, that I'm quite shattered by it. Of the magic
of his eye you can form no notion : if only he be
granted life ; it is too rare a miracle!

Hearty friendship to Wille and the young men !

Ever   Your grateful
                    RICHARD WAGNER.

Spread nothing abroad! Not a word to the
papers! Everything is private, and must remain
so !—

5.

STARNBERG IN BAVARIA, 26*th May* 1864.

My very dear and honoured Friend,

Indeed I doubt that this letter will catch you
at Mariafeld, but I presume it will be sent on to you.
I really am simply writing to prevent the thought
arising in you, that I could be unthankful to you.
At your house I had to surmount the fearful labour-
pains of my good-fortune, and you were my mid-
wife : we saw and felt nothing but the awe and

anguish of that birth; thus may it be with actual mothers a fight 'twixt life and death, where the thought of that which is to be born fades out entirely for the while, and the pangs alone are left as reality. Yet I hardly know how I could have endured it all and finally been able to bid goodbye to you in tolerable self-possession on the whole, tho' without any visible hope, if there had not lurked in my being's depths a sort of consciousness that my un-precedented sufferings at least *had won me a title to some higher import,* and a title which, even if not conceded by the world, yet raised me so much higher above the world, and thus, albeit in deepest misery, *made me inwardly a charmed and blessed man.*

You, dear friend, can bear witness that I have a right to rate my sufferings thus high. Reflect, to what a depth I was abased. Farther it surely could not go? And truly—so far had it gone! But see, priceless friend! this deepest humbling has raised me at last: I felt that, if it had been possible for me to bear this, and yet stay meek and kindly, there must be something higher meant with me. Like lightning it flashed through me, that the curtain must suddenly rise, and some wondrous happiness be shewn to me. *You felt so, too;* plainly did you speak it out. Avow it, we both were as if inspired by God. Friend, and *this* was my feeling: whether the curtain would lift in this life, or only with death, indeed was all one to *me:* that lift it would, I knew. —So it came that, when my wondrous happiness arrived, I was not at all affrighted: of itself I had

been perfectly sure ; merely the drastic swiftness of
its entry, exactly now, on this very day, at this hour,
—that startled me. The envoy was with me at the
moment when letters came in from Vienna, reporting
the most abominable consequences of the disastrous
step of my friends and representatives, so that I
decided to set off at once for Vienna. My envoy
accompanied me to Munich, where I had to spend
the night as I had missed the right train, and the
next morning I was hindered by terrible sickness
from continuing my journey that day. However,
I pulled myself sufficiently together to visit the
young King after midday. At once all was clear
and appointed : the curtain was drawn up. After a
few days I pursued my journey to Vienna ; what
nothing but the despairing energy of personal sacri-
fice could have accomplished erewhile, was now an
easy business to arrange. I came back with my
servants [a married couple] and my faithful hound
to my new last home, where, borne by the divinest
love, I now enjoy the wondrous fortune we gave
birth to in that fever-night at Mariafeld.

Have no doubt of this, my dear. This is the
fortune which alone can fully balance all the sorrows
I have had to bear with to the utmost misery. I
feel that, had it not arrived, I should yet have
deserved it : and that affords me warrant of its
lasting. However, if you would learn the credentials
of the godlike origin of *this* good luck, you now shall
hear them. In the year of the first performance of my
" Tannhäuser" (the work with which I first entered

my new and thorny path), in the month (August) in which I felt impelled to such excessive productivity that I sketched the "Lohengrin" and "Meistersinger" at like time, a mother bore my guardian angel.

At the time when I had just finished my "Tristan" at Lucerne, was straining every nerve to gain the possibility of settlement on German soil (Baden), and turned at last to Paris in despair, there to wear myself out with undertakings against my nature—in his 15th year the youth was attending his first performance of my "Lohengrin," which took such hold of him that he thenceforth drew his self-tuition from the study of my works and writings, and has openly declared to his entourage, as now to me, that *I* have been his sole true teacher and bringer-up. He follows my career and hardships, the Parisian atrocities, my ruin in Germany, and cherishes one only wish, to gain the power to prove the height of his affection to me. It was the youth's one, truly devouring grief, not to know how to win from his obtuse environment that needful interest in me. At the beginning of *last* March, I know the day, the miscarriage of every attempt to mend my broken state grew clear to me : in helpless despair I looked with open eyes toward all that was so horribly degradingly arriving. Then the King of Bavaria dies—quite unexpectedly—and my compassionate guardian angel—against all rules of Fate—ascends a throne. His earliest care a month thereafter, is to send for me : while I am draining the cup of sorrow to its lowest dregs, with your merciful aid, the envoy already is seeking me in my deserted home at Penzing ; he must bring the King a pen, a pencil from me.—How and when he found me at last, you know. —My dear, no doubt is possible here :—*That* was it, and *that* it is !—Ah ! at last a tie that brings with it no pains and tortures ! What it is for me, to have this glorious youth before me ! On my birthday he presented me with a beautiful oil-portrait, for which he had sat expressly for me. This wonderful picture has taught me how to shew to others, too, that I have " genius " : there, see there, you have my " Genius " before your eyes !—

An intimate friend of the King's has assured me that it seems to him the youth is so strict and serious in matters of government merely so as to avoid the influence of anyone, and thus secure himself the fullest liberty and independence to live for his love to me. He is thoroughly aware who I am, and what I need : not a word have I had to waste about my situation. He feels that a King's prerogative must assuredly suffice to keep all common cares from me, to give me altogether to my Muse, and procure me every means to produce my works when and how I wish. At present he mostly resides in a little castle near to me ; in 10 minutes the carriage takes me there. Daily he sends either once or twice. Then I fly as to a sweetheart. 'Tis a fascinating interview. This thirst for instruction, this comprehension, this quiver and glow, I have never encountered in such splendid unrestraint. And then this charming care for me, this winning chastity of heart, of every feature, when he assures me of his happiness in possessing me : thus do we often sit for hours together, lost in each other's gaze. He makes no parade of me : we are altogether for ourselves. If I would—so they tell me—the whole Court might stand free to me : He would not understand me, if I asked for an ambitious rôle there. So beautiful and genuine is it all.—How easy is it for me thus to tranquillise on every hand : I am not remarked, I injure no one ; everything, what we both despise at heart, pursues the even tenour of its way ; we trouble not for that. In time they all will like me ; already the immediate entourage of the young King is happy to find and know me *thus*, since each perceives that my enormous influence on the prince's mind can only tend to good, to no one's harm. Thus everything both in and round us turns better and more beautiful each day !—

This is my fortune, Friend ! Do you doubt its being the right one ? The right, ah ! yes—the right it must be : now you shall see how it lasts, and how all prospers. Have no doubt !

(Written a few days later.)

If one thing in my life has utterly prostrated me, it is an attribute of the " world " against which your humble servant can do just nothing. This is the philistine-soul's conceit in its "practical good sense," its often blandly smiling claim to exclusive wisdom when confronted with the rare deep spirits it cannot fathom. This ghastly shrewdness, this ridiculous bluntness in the valuation of the things of life, which now and then brings off its triumphs over the fantastic madcap,—when faced with the really deeper spirit it falls to nothing, speaking strictly, but the animal instinct for discovering the useful for the mere day's need ; since the deeper spirit constantly, and often purposely, neglects this primarily-needful —not to allow itself to be disturbed in its wider gaze,—to that practical world-cleverness it seems absurd and absolutely unintelligible. Well, we must put up with the fact that the world, which *we* comprehend well enough, doesn't comprehend us, and permits itself to commiserate our unpractical nature. When this relation is transferred to the sphere of Morality, however, and the Philistine upholds himself as the only moral person, simply because he neither comprehends nor has any feeling for *true* morality, then deference and ironical admission of the rightness of the other side become hard indeed. But when a *woman's* heart so forgets every instinct of love, that she judges the object of her love by this philistine standard of ethics, commiserates, and— exhorts, it can no longer be suffered. My having so petted and spoilt my own wife by excessive indulgence, that at last she lost all power of rendering me a little justice, has become to me a nemesis. The result has appeared. — — —

Where are you now, dear friend? Won't you write me once again? I'm quite lonely here : I lack a little company in the house ; perhaps I shall get Cornelius to come. Shall I be able to do entirely without the " womanly " ? With such a deep sigh I say No, that I almost must wish it !—One glance at his dear picture helps again ! Ah, this adorable youth ! Of a truth he is all to me, world, wife and child !

A thousand cordial wishes ! Ever yours,
R. WAGNER.

————

6.

STARNBERG IN BAVARIA, 30*th* *June* 1864.

Dear, precious Friend,

I am very tired, and suffering from what I have passed through : now that the excitement is abating, the pain steps in, as with wounds. Not so quickly as you might suppose, shall I be at my art again. The thought of how things would stand with me now, if this One and Unexpected had not happened, still makes me marvel ; for all I once believed I might expect, both has and would have lamentably failed me ! That I now review, and shudder.—My solitude is terrible. Only as on a highest mountain-peak, can I maintain my stand with this young King. The forlornness of my household, the obligation to concern my solitary

self with things for which I never was made, lames
my vital spirits : I have had to undergo another
removal, to arrange an establishment, to worry myself about knives, forks, dishes and saucepans, bed-
clothes, etc. I, the glorifier of women ! How
kindly they repay me, by leaving me their business !—

Dearest friend, the most beautiful thing in your
beautiful letter is the suggestion of your visit ! For
it I now hope, and therefore write you nothing
more ; which suits my fatigue very well. You
would be splendidly off here : I've a whole large
house to myself, as I couldn't avoid it, and you shall
find everything to your convenience. Bring an
amanuensis with you, and dictate your promised
novel while you dine. We really must have a good
long talk *for once* again : who knows when we may
have another ! So gladly would I die now !—

Yesterday Frau v. Bülow arrived, with 2
children and nursemaid : the husband will follow.
That livens somewhat ; yet such is my mood, that
nothing more will make a right impression. Perhaps the bad weather is alone to blame—don't you
agree with me ? We artists surely don't take any
other thing so seriously ! Well, that we shall discover. Only come soon, and stay a long time.
About my young King, just this one word more :
if I really am not wholly and entirely happy, it is not
his fault. Of the magnificence of this relation you
certainly have not a full idea as yet. That you will
have to obtain on the spot ; in short—the male sex

has completely re-established itself in my eyes through this its representative.—

All this you will see!—Adieu! dear, precious carer, guardian, deep-seer!—A thousand thanks for your friendship!

From my heart   Your

R. Wagner.

7.

Starnberg, 9th September 1864.

Dear, precious Friend,

I turn to you once more, to have a little chat with you, as I have so often had at heart of late. —Indeed it wasn't nice of you, not to have paid me a visit : yet I know full well that with you nothing takes precedence over house, husband and children, and consequently you belong to the absolutely happy, those-who possess this wholly, or at least in part, and prove at each forthcoming option that no soever happiness excels the one which they possess,—therefore Absolutely-happy!

Well, to them I *don't* belong. Just figure how it goes with me :—complete life-weariness is struggling in me with the conscious purpose to employ my life aright at last. With Purpose—singular to say!—'tis never well with me : I observe that there it all is strictly affectation, nothing sound behind. And this is the cause that a profound disbelief in my life often reveals itself again to me in sweetly soothing guise : then there are moments, as on dropping off to sleep, when one tastes of true felicity.—

However, I have a young King who really loves
me to distraction : you cannot form a notion of it !
I remember a dream from my earliest youth, where
I dreamt that Shakespeare was alive and I was looking
at and speaking with him, truly, in the flesh ; its
impression was never to be forgotten, and passed into
the yearning to see Beethoven too (who also was
already dead). Something similar must be taking
place in this delightful being, when he has me with
him. He tells me he can scarcely yet believe he has
me really !—No one can read his letters to me without awe and enchantment. Liszt considered that
in them he stood on a fully equal grade of receptivity
with my own productivity. 'Tis a miracle !—
Believe it !—And that should not make one glad ?
It must indeed ! Yet—how hard, how hard does
gladness come to me ! Nothing less than this wonderful King must it have been, else were it—finished,
absolutely finished !

So had I *really been abandoned* by all my *old
friends :*—literally *you* alone still believed in me.—

Since a while I have been quite alone again, as in
some haunted castle. I won't deny that this total
solitude is now becoming very harmful to me :
believe me, 'tis an ailment of which I shall bleed
away. Unfortunately things were just as crooked
before, when I had friends with me : there was
neither blessing nor peace. At the beginning of
July poor Bülow came in the most worn-out condition, with overwrought and shattered nerves, found
bad cold weather all the time, consequently an un-

healthy climate, and fell from one attack of illness into another. Add to it a tragic marriage ; a young, most exceptionally gifted wife, the very image of Liszt, but intellectually his superior.— Were I but made so as to skim my share of agreeables from the surface of things ! That I am not, however ; I'm foolish enough to take everything so seriously. The most urgent measure, was to snatch Bülow from his insanely exhausting employment, and supply him with a nobler field.

It was easy to move the young King—for whom, again, it was highly important—to appoint Bülow as his chamber-player. So I am hoping to have the Bülows with me here for good, ere long. On both I have impressed that there is but one means of redemption for us all : the highest art-creating and working in common.—We then should have one reason more for holding out and striking in,—in spite of all the hardships of life-weariness.—You see, nothing with me goes off smoothly ! Not even a case such as Lassalle's death : the unhappy man was here (through Bülow) exactly 14 days before, to seek my intervention with the King of Bavaria against his Minister in Switzerland, Dönnigues. (For I simply am thought an all-powerful minion : the other day the orphans of a female poisoner appealed to me !) What do you say to it ? I didn't know Lassalle at all ; on this occasion he heartily mis-pleased me : it was a love-story of rampant vanity and false pathos. In him I beheld the type of the men of consequence in our near future, which I can

only call the Germano-Judaic.—I am still without a
dwelling in town : I should like to have something
that promises permanence, and cannot find it. I'm
to have something built for me : but that will take
two years. Shall I really live as long ? And yet I
must. My young King is saving, discontinuing his
father's building-plans, etc., to keep the money for
representation of the Nibelungen. As yet I haven't
had one day of real old rest : I'm hesitating what to
take up first. Perhaps I shall set everything else on
one side, and complete the Nibelungen : if I say that
to the King, I am still better off.—

But listen : the 2nd October, for the King's first
reappearance in the theatre, I set before him a
model performance of the "Flying Dutchman"
(alas ! the only one of all my operas that *can* be
given well at present). Everything is prepared for
a completely good performance. Middle of October
I have a grand concert, with my new fragments, as
at Carlsruhe before.[1] Will you come ?—*May* next
year " Tristan " with the Schnorrs.—Will you come
then too ?

How stands it with the *novel* ?—How goes it with
Wille and the sons ? Please greet them most kindly
from me.—What's going on in the " accursed
neighbourhood " ?[2] Have they remained friends

---

[1] The 14th and 19th November 1863.
[2] " Verwünschte Gegend "—this *might* be rendered the " enchanted land," but
as it evidently refers to the " green hill," I believe it must be taken in con-
junction with the addendum to the letter of May 26, and therefore is a quotation
from some letter of Minna Wagner's, whose jealousy had already broken up the
master's home in 1858.—Tr.

with me? Do they believe in my gratitude? Do *you* believe in me?—Answer before the concert. Hearty greetings!

Your

R. WAGNER.

8.

MUNICH, 21 BRIENNERSTRASSE, 8*th* *Oct.* '64.

Precious!

Your silence alarms me. Surely you received a letter of mine a short while back?—

I am adopting a means of extorting a speedy answer from you.

I enclose a letter of my young King's to me, and beg you to return it as soon as possible, as a pledge in trust!—

Yesterday, when we settled the completion and performance of my Nibelungen, I was so awe-struck by this heavenly prodigy of a royal youth, that I came near to sinking on my knees and worshipping him.—

Beginning of November, Flying Dutchman and performance of my fragments (with Schnorr).— Spring : Tristan. Summer 1867 : Nibelungenring. A thousand greetings!

From my heart   Your

R. WAGNER.

9.

Dear Lady,

Two words to shew you how the land lies! My Refutation you know :[1] here it is again. It contains one subterfuge : touching the limitedness of my relations with the King. For my need of repose I heartily wish that they were so. This wonderfully deep and fatalistic liking of the King for me,—if (for peace' sake) I renounce the rights it gives me, I cannot yet reconcile it with my heart, my conscience, to shuffle off the duties it imposes on me. You may guess that those set on to me in public are mere tools : this has no consequence, and calumny already is playing its last despairing stake. But the motives? I can but shudder at the thought of withdrawing within the bounds demanded by my own repose, and leaving *him*—to *his* surroundings.—

I quake in the depths of my soul, and ask my dæmon : Why this cup?—Why, when I sought for rest and leisure undisturbed for work, am I involved in a responsibility which places in my hands the weal of a divinely-gifted human being, perhaps the welfare of a land?—How save my heart here? How still be artist too?—*He lacks every man he needs!*—This, this is my veritable torment. The

---

[1] In reply to an article in the *Allg. Ztg.* of Feb. 19, 1865. Wagner's Refutation is dated Feb. 20, and appeared in the *Allg. Ztg.* of Feb. 22, 1865 ; for its full text, see my preface to Vol. IV. of the *Prose Works*, pp. ix to xv The author must have had a singularly tender conscience, to see a lack of candour—"*Unaufrichtigkeit*"—in his not affording the gapers a full account of his intimacy with Ludwig II.—W. A. E.

outward game of intrigue, simply reckoned to throw me off my balance, and draw from me an indiscretion, easily recoils on itself. But what an energy, destructive of my peace for ever, should I require to snatch my youthful friend forever from his entourage! —He keeps loyal, touchingly true to me, and shuts himself just now from everyone.—

What do you say to my fate?—My yearning for the last repose is unspeakable : my heart can't bear this dizziness much longer!—

Hearty greetings to Wille!

Entirely your faithful
RICHARD WAGNER.

MUNICH, 26th February 1865.

10.

Dearest Lady,

A miracle! I really have an hour's rest and good spirits, which I am spending on a dozen letters. Yours has this moment arrived : so 2 to 3 lines must you have, that's of course, though Cosima had promised me to write you also in my name.—Yet it surely is not possible for you to believe that I have not daily thought of you at *this* time with fondness, thanks and sorrow? Certainly not! Every blade of grass in my garden recalls the turning green of yours a year ago.

So then—*come!* You see, it is your husband bids

me soundly rate you! Eh! but that's fine!—how heartily I've had to laugh at Wille!—

Yes, come! May 15th, 18th and 22nd[1] are the three performances in chief. They will be *wonderful*, as *never* seen. For that had I to suffer, that to see! Of the splendour of the two Schnorrs you can form no conception! All the strength of their lives is concentrated on this one achievement, which they now are compassing with full artistic honour.—My article is all too poor in its description of the circumstances in which I am bringing my work to light.[2] Of the divineness of my youthful King no hymn could sing exhaustively. Here everything is like a fairy-dream; one cannot credit that such beauty, depth, sublimity, should suddenly appear in human life. And how wise he is, without knowing it in the slightest. But much of sorrow hovers o'er us : the fearful meanness of the entourage and all surroundings,—and yet all governed wisely by him, with quite infallible instinct.—God,—if *he* but thrive and prosper! Then, at last, the German nation has for once the pattern that it needs—an other than Friedrich II.

All my fears have lightly been dispelled by *His* inimitable certainty of feeling. Naught harms him —he is charmed.

---

[1] Owing to the illness of Frau Schnorr (the "Isolde") *Tristan* had eventually to be postponed to June 8th for the so-called "dress-rehearsal" (in reality a private representation), the public performances taking place on June 10th, 13th and 19th, and July 1st, 1865.

[2] The "Invitation to the Production of Tristan in Munich" published in the *Wiener Botschafter*, April 1865 ; this will presently appear in Vol. VIII. of the *Prose Works*.

The heartiest greetings to Wille! Be ashamed of yourself—and come ; 't will be worth the while. From my whole heart

Your

R. WAGNER.

31st April,[1] 1865.

II.

MUNICH, *26th Sept.* 1865.

Say, my dear Friend, how was it possible for you thus to pass me by, this summer? How often have I wanted to address that question to you! Amazement always held me back.—It was possible to you, not even to follow your husband's persuasion! So then : with me you lived through terrible and startling epochs of my life in closest confidence, with me you felt and suffered, to cut me suddenly adrift at one important climax!—How strange! What can one think of it ?—

Now what shall I tell you of myself ?—

I spoke of an "important climax" : I did not say a "joyful" one. That even here, at this height, but pain and sorrow were sincerely to be felt for me, —did you guess that, perhaps, and feel too suffering yourself to spare me your pity ?—

There was a brief interval when I really thought I must be dreaming, so wonderfully beautiful 'twas round my heart. It was the time of the rehearsals for "Tristan."

[1] I cannot substitute "30th April" for this date, as it was probably May 1, and Wagner may have used it deliberately as in Letter 53 to Uhlig, where he dates "53rd December '51" with an explanation.—W. A. E.

To Frau Eliza Wille   165

For the first time in my life, with my whole full art I here was if on a pillow of Love. So must it be for once! Noble, grand, ample and free, the whole equipment of the studio : a wonderful pair of artists, bestowed by heaven, inwardly versed and most fondly devoted, gifted to astonishment. My faithful guardian-angel ever floating over me with beauty and blessing, full of childlike glee at my content, my joy at the growing achievement : ever ordering unseen what served me, removing what was cumbrous to me. Like a magic dream throve the work to unequalled reality : the first performance—without public, merely for ourselves—given out as dress-rehearsal, resembled the fulfilment of the Impossible.

The sense of dreaming never left me : I marvelled and marvelled—how 'twere possible to live to this! —This was the splendid climax, and yet *embittered* by—*absences!*—Of a truth : embittered! How small you all appear to me, you who—shunned this agitation!—

Thenceforth—nothing but sorrow. As I really pay no more heed to so-called "success," all such seeming experiments before the public to me were simply ruffling and derogatory. At the fourth performance—in the last act—I was seized by a feeling of the sacrilege of this unheard achievement : I cried, This is the last performance of Tristan, never must it be given again. And I was taken at my word. My glorious singer left us cheering, glad and happy in his pride and wellbeing. A week thereafter I tore to Dresden, to be present at his burial :

pyæmia[1] they called the demon that had flown from his knee to his brain. There he lay.—Since then my outlook is a sad one. I was lonely in the lofty hills, and I am lonely here. I cannot bear to speak with anyone, and pass for out of town. The wonderful affection of the King keeps me to life : he cares for me as never man cared for another. In him I revive, and for him will I still create my works. For myself I, strictly speaking, live no more. Yet He keeps everything aloof from me, that would remind me of life and actuality : henceforth I can do nothing but dream and create.

So it goes, and will go. My passion for work absorbs all my thoughts. The Nibelungen shall now be finished : a Parzival is drafted already. It all is fabulous, dreamlike : else all were deadly painful.

Now tell me your news.—A thousand greetings, dear trusty friend! Do you still recall your prophecies? Ah, but no matter : what of them could be fulfilled, has been fulfilled as never aught before—more beautiful than any dream. And you will not even draw near the habitation of that dream?

My best and kindest wishes to all, from
Your
RICHARD WAGNER.

---

[1] "*Springende Gicht*," literally "flying gout," or "rheumatic fever"; but I should imagine the above diagnosis to be the more correct.—W. A. E.

12.

GENEVA, *Campagne des "Artichauts,"* 26th Dec. 1865.

Dear honoured Lady!
   You see, I am taking everything quite seriously, and certainly you also expect me to abide by the seriousness of my last letter to you. Accept my sincere and deep-felt thanks for your answer. I have merely waited for the time which you announced as your return to Mariafeld, to write again, as you requested, what my final decision might be.—I remain, what I was.—

   About my Munich complications I can tell you little : you must be able to clear the lying vapours for yourself, if you want to see. I'm taking every single thing quite seriously, and of worldly wisdom there can be no talk with me. At the moment it is requisite to leave the young King time to learn to rule a little and be Master. The school of present sufferings will be good for him. His too great love for me had made him blind to all other relations around him : so that he was easy to dupe. He reads nobody,—and must begin to learn mankind. But I have hope for him. Just as I am sure of his love for ever, do I also trust to the development of his splendid parts. He only needs to learn to know men rather better. Then he will soon hit the mark.

Send me your " Felicitas," and don't treat my
request for it as cajolery !—
Fare you well !   Many greetings to Wille.
                    Your
                        RICHARD WAGNER.

———

There follows a gap of over three years, in which
epistolary correspondence with Frau Wille would appear to
have ceased, save for an invitation to the *Meistersinger ;*
in fact she tells us (*Rundschau,* March '87) that she had
purposely abstained from going to either Starnberg or the
Munich *Tristan,* as she somewhat disapproved (!) of Wagner's
influence with the King.   However, the master spent a few
days at Mariafeld at some period, unspecified, after his settling
down at Tribschen.   Into his own movements meanwhile,
it is unnecessary to inquire here ; they are partly indicated
by other letters in this little book, but a full account belongs
to a biography proper.

13.

Dear honoured Friend,
           Your kind good letter has much rejoiced me.
—According to a promise which you gave us 2
years back, for some time past we had been expecting a longish visit of yours to Tribschen.   Last
summer I long hoped for its fulfilment, and was not
indisposed to form glum thoughts about your non-
arrival.

Since then I haven't left my retreat, and think of
stopping here for years without budging, firmly re-
solved to devote myself to nothing but my labours,
not to any more fruitless and fatiguing efforts without. At the present moment I am busy finishing
the Siegfried, broken off in 1858.[1]—

My noble ministering friend is here with her
children, where she has been with me for some time.
We see nobody, but should be glad to welcome
you.

Your greeting [birthday] has done me good.
Stay friends with me, and be of good cheer. You
deserve a shining crown.

From my heart   Your
                                            RICHARD WAGNER.

TRIBSCHEN, 25*th May* 1869.

14.

Dear honoured Friend,
        I take the liberty of recalling myself to your
memory by sending you a new brochure of mine—
this time " About Conducting."—Some things in it

---

[1] This date, of course, is incorrect; it should be " 1857." However, it
possibly is either a misprint, or a mistake in copying the letter for the press, since
the date of the letter itself is incorrectly given by Frau Wille as 1868. Internal
evidence proves this last to be an error, for Wagner was at that time busy re-
hearsing the *Meistersinger* for its first performances in June; moreover, in a
reminiscence which she locates *before* this Letter 13, Frau Wille herself tells us
that she received an invitation from Frau v. Bülow to the *Meistersinger* in 1868,
and that, accepting it, she spent a day with Wagner and the Bülows at Munich.
Lastly, the remark about " finishing Siegfried " stamps this as 1869, as may be
seen from the letter of Aug. 21 to Wesendonck.—W. A. E.

will interest you. Perhaps, however, some will also give a slight offence—if not exactly in your house, yet elsewhere at Zurich ; wherefore I withhold the booklet from another quarter.

You see, I stand to my guns and don't lose heart, though every hope.

With the heartiest greetings and most grateful remembrances, Your faithful

RICHARD WAGNER.

LUCERNE, 26th March 1870.

———

15.

Dear honoured Friend,

I hardly need to tell you what delight your letter and your invitation have afforded us !—Of course we will come, for you shall be the first to whom we introduce ourselves as man and wife. To arrive at this state has cost great patience : what for years has been indispensable, was only to be compassed under sufferings of every kind. Since I saw you last in Munich, I have not left my refuge, to which since then She also fled who had to testify that it was feasible to help me, and thus disprove the axiom of so many of my friends, that I " could not be helped." She knew that help could be extended me, and helped she has : She has braved opprobrium and taken every blame upon herself. She has borne me a marvellously beautiful and sturdy son, whom I could proudly christen "Siegfried": so he is thriving with my work, and gives me a new lease of life, which *finally has found a meaning.*—

Thus have we shifted for ourselves, without a "world" from which we had retired completely. And so has staunchness been approved, and more affecting than the gain of new friends has been the loyalty of old ones. My sister Ottilie Brockhaus visited us as long ago as last late-summer, with her family : I heartily wished you had been here. But now St. John's day brings you to us. Our cordial welcome !

Yet listen : you may deem it right and sensible, that we should not pursue your invitation till I can lead to you the mother of my son as furthermore my wedded wife. That isn't far off now, and we hope to step into Mariafeld before the leaf falls. But prove me your whole true friendship, and with your admirable family come soon, right soon before, to us at Tribschen. If you have grandchildren, do bring them too ; here you will find a troop of youth that musters merrily around its mother, who is alike its teacher and its bringer-up. Beyond that, maybe much else to give you joy.

How deeply and how earnestly should we rejoice, if you announced yourself right soon ! Any day is right to us ; we're always ready.—

You prophesied it to me, noble one ! Don't you remember, when you sped me from your hospitable roof six years ago ? I was wretched. But you looked at me, and—augured,—you surely recollect !

Well, friend ! now come and convince yourself that you have the right heart for a good prophetess !

All blessings on you ! May everything thrive whereon your great, grand heart is set ! This my return salute !—

Your
RICHARD WAGNER.

TRIBSCHEN, 25*th June* 1870.

Richard and Cosima Wagner were married at Lucerne on the 25th August, 1870, King Ludwig's twenty-fifth birthday. The Willes paid their first visit on September 3.

[With the above this correspondence ceases, but a budget of letters to Emil Heckel, one of the " new friends," takes up the story of the master's life from 1871 to 1883, the year of his death.]

Index

In the following I have adopted a plan which I have found to work fairly well with my indexes to *Richard Wagner's Prose Works*, viz. figures denoting the tens and hundreds are not repeated for one and the same reference unless the numerals should happen to run into a fresh line of type : thus

"*Meistersinger* poem, 93, 5, 127, 34, 8," will stand for
Meistersinger poem, see pages 93, 95, 127, 134 and 138.

References to footnotes will bear the letter "*n*" after the numeral.—W. A. E.

THE END

Printed by R. & R. Clark, Limited, *Edinburgh*.

For EU product safety concerns, contact us at Calle de José Abascal, 56–1°, 28003 Madrid, Spain or eugpsr@cambridge.org.

www.ingramcontent.com/pod-product-compliance
Ingram Content Group UK Ltd.
Pitfield, Milton Keynes, MK11 3LW, UK
UKHW040616240426
470322UK00010B/154